The Beatitudes

The Beatitudes

Seeking the Joy of God's Kingdom

Paul Hinnebusch, OP

Pauline

BOOKS & MEDIA

Boston

Library of Congress Cataloging-in-Publication Data

Hinnebusch, Paul.
  The Beatitudes : seeking the joy of God's kingdom / Paul
Hinnebusch.
      p. cm.
  Includes bibliographical references.
  ISBN 0-8198-1153X (paper)
     1. Beatitudes—Criticism, interpretation, etc. 2. Poverty—
Biblical teaching. I. Title.

BT382 .H56 2000
241.5'3—dc21   99–056251

Cover design: Helen Rita Lane, FSP

Printed and published in the U.S.A. by Pauline Books & Media,
50 Saint Pauls Avenue, Boston MA 02130-3491.

www.pauline.org

Pauline Books & Media is the publishing house of the Daughters
of St. Paul, an international congregation of women religious
serving the Church with the communications media.

1 2 3 4 5 6   05 04 03 02 01 00

Contents

Contents

PART THREE
THE EIGHT BEATITUDES

Foreword

As a first reader of this manuscript prior to publication, and as one familiar with the author's style, I offer a few suggestions on how to most fully benefit from this book.

First of all, buy it! Buy several, one to keep at hand to turn to often, others to loan and give as gifts. I say this with a firm conviction that this book will make a tremendous difference in your spiritual life.

Second, do not plunge immediately into part three in eagerness to devour what the author has to say on the beatitudes. Do not skip over or browse through parts one and two. This is not solely a book on the beatitudes, but a guide to happiness in God. Part one on the *anawim,* and part two on Mary, distinguishes this treatise from other works on the beatitudes. It is also distinguished by the author's extraordinary understanding of righteousness and living in the kingdom of God, in union with God's saving will. Fr. Hinnebusch begins from the premise that the spirituality of the *anawim* is so intrinsic to Christian spirituality that we cannot live the beatitudes until we become *anawim.* Thus, we cannot grasp the author's definition of Christian spirituality nor his explanation of the beatitudes without thoroughly digesting his message on the spirituality of the *anawim,* exemplified by Mary.

This foundational background may well be the missing link to accessing the power of Jesus' central teaching on the beatitudes. Many Christians, myself included, for want of this link have erroneously relegated the beatitudes to some peripheral role. Some have thought the beatitudes demand too high a perfection. Others have known the beatitudes should be central to our life in God, but simply have not known how to make them so. All this can be remedied by grasping the Spirit-filled originality Fr. Hinnebusch uses to help us understand the beatitudes as Christian spirituality itself, the spirituality of the *anawim*. So do not view part three on the beatitudes as the main course. This book has many main courses. Linger at its feast.

Third, read patiently. Allow the light of deeper union with God to fill you ray by ray, sentence by sentence. This book is both a guide for spiritual growth and an in-depth Scripture study. As a Scripture scholar and a Dominican theologian well versed in Church tradition, Fr. Hinnebusch intersperses relevant ideas from St. Thomas Aquinas along with Scripture passages. He integrates concepts into a global view of fundamental truths, while polishing and illuminating related details like multiple facets of a jewel. The author's artistry in weaving together scriptural truths is both spiral and cyclical. A concept expounded and summarized may later be reexamined in light of further teaching, then resummarized to connect it with another facet of a new idea.

Such richness could be mistaken for repetition by a hurried reader accustomed to today's fast pace. However, this stylistic element is the author's strength. Each return to a concept rewards the patient reader with new ideas that contribute to a greater understanding of the whole.

Finally, read prayerfully, daring to enter the still quietude where God speaks. Since the book is a fruit of the author's prayer life, it will best bear fruit in us when read in an attitude of attentive prayer. Listen to the Holy Spirit's enlightenment about the personal relevance of each beatitude. The author gives helpful practical applications drawn from years as a spiritual director and minister of the sacrament of Reconciliation. He shows us common pitfalls and misunderstandings. His treatment of the beatitudes reveals to us how a person is formed in virtue. The author's analysis of various biblical terms and scriptural themes related to the beatitudes leads the reader to a fresh vision of how the beatitudes work together.

This book will be a classic addition to the Christian library. Without realizing it, Fr. Hinnebusch has exposed his soul to us. In his latest book, this well acclaimed author has distilled for us the wisdom of his extensive scholarship, over fifty years of ministry, and a life of contemplative prayer. Return to it repeatedly to meditate on the beatitudes as a way of life, that "dynamic posture" from which all our living should spring. May all who do so receive the blessing, the *beatitude,* of living in the Father's joy in the kingdom of God on earth, then in heaven. *Marantha!* Come, Lord Jesus!

Celine Maria Powers, TOC

Preface

Recently the Ecumenical Program of Christian Spirituality in Dallas invited me to speak on the beatitudes as the moral foundation of Christian spirituality. In preparing these teachings for the program, I soon realized that the beatitudes are not merely the moral foundation of Christian spirituality; they are Christian spirituality itself. Anyone who fully lives the beatitudes lives the fullness of Christian spirituality.

But more than that, such a person is living Israel's spirituality in its full flowering, namely, the spirituality of the *anawim*, Yahweh's poor ones. To live the beatitudes that Jesus presented is to live this spirituality to the full.

The spirituality of the *anawim* is openness to the messiah. Christians believe that Jesus is the messiah. He came not to destroy the law, but to fulfill it (cf. Mt 5:17). He did not abrogate Israel's *Torah*, but brought it to its highest perfection. In saying, "I desire mercy, not sacrifice" (Mt 9:13; 12:7), he was renewing the call to fidelity to the covenant with the Lord. "Mercy," we shall see, translates the Hebrew word *ḥesed*, meaning "covenant fidelity."

One can be a true Christian only by living this spirituality of the *anawim*, which is receptivity to the messiah. The beatitudes, the spirituality of the *anawim*, do not just prepare for Christian spirituality or provide a moral foundation for it; they *are* this spirituality. They can be lived in their fullness only in the power of the Holy Spirit given by Jesus, the messiah. Life in the Spirit is the life of the beatitudes.

These points gradually became evident to me as the writing progressed. At first I tried to concentrate on the moral aspects of the beatitudes, but soon realized that this would not treat them adequately. The teaching presented in the book evolved over a period of several months. In preparing for the Ecumenical Program, I first presented the material in a series of talks given to Mother Teresa's Missionaries of Charity in Dallas. This more leisurely presentation allowed an evolution of thought that would not otherwise have taken place.

Plan of the Book

The book has three sections. The first briefly presents the spirituality of the *anawim*. The second presents the Blessed Virgin Mary as the best model of this spirituality. As spokesperson of the *anawim,* Mary sings her Magnificat in their language. The third section treats each of the eight beatitudes in the light of *anawim* spirituality, with the help of words of Jesus from the rest of Matthew's Gospel, and as illustrated from the life of Jesus himself.

The beatitudes express eight different facets of one complex relationship with God. One needs to understand all the beatitudes in order to understand any one of them. So whatever is said about a particular beatitude is not confined to the chapter dedicated to that one. In nearly every chapter something is said about each of the eight, since all eight illumine different aspects of one relationship with God. To live any one of them is to live them all.

Acknowledgments

I thank the Missionaries of Charity for being such responsive listeners. Your listening hearts invited the grace of God that was at work in the preparation of this book. I also thank you, students at the Ecumenical Program. Your gratifying response to my teaching encouraged me to write this book.

Mrs. Celine Powers, a participant in the Ecumenical Program, attended my original lecture on the beatitudes. As the first person to read the draft of this book, she critiqued it from two points of view: the literary and the inspirational. Out of her background as a teacher of literary composition, she made many valuable suggestions. From her deep experience of Christian living, she greatly enriched my understanding of the practical living of the beatitudes, and helped me to speak more effectively to the everyday experience of those who will read this book. As she pointed out, my approach is that of a theologian and exegete, striving for clarity of thought, while she takes this approach: What do the readers need to hear? What speaks best to their experience of life?

At Mrs. Powers' suggestion, I made many additions to the book that aim at showing how the beatitude promised by Christ is to be experienced not just in the world to come, but here and now. She helped me to bring this book "down to earth."

I am deeply grateful to Celine Powers for her loving, painstaking reading of the original manuscript and for her excellent suggestions. I also wish to thank Mrs. Katherine C. Rogers for her many services facilitating the publication of this work, especially for preparing the diskettes for the publisher. Thanks also to Sr. M. Lorraine Trouvé, FSP, who edited it for publication.

Select Bibliography

The points made in chapter one, "The Holy Remnant," were gleaned chiefly from:

Vawter, Bruce. *The Conscience of Israel.* New York: Sheed & Ward, 1961.

Chapter two, a brief sketch of *anawim* spirituality, was inspired chiefly by:

Gelin, Albert. *The Poor of Yahweh.* Collegeville: The Liturgical Press, 1964.

Chapter three, "'The Proud' Versus 'The Poor,'" was guided by:

Brennan, Joseph P. "Psalms 1–8: Some Hidden Harmonies." *Biblical Theology Bulletin* 10 (1980): pp. 25–29.

Chapter four, "The Poor One Par Excellence," a commentary on Psalm 22, is based upon:

Stuhlmueller, Carroll. *Psalms I,* Old Testament Message, vol. 21. Wilmington: Glazier, 1983, pp. 144–151.

Part two, "The Virgin Mary: Spokesperson of the *Anawim,*" is based on commentaries on the Magnificat found in:

Brown, Raymond E. *The Birth of the Messiah.* New York: Doubleday, 1977, pp. 355–365.
Johnson, Luke Timothy. *Sacra Pagina: The Gospel of Luke.* Collegeville: Glazier, 1991, pp. 40–43. I have borrowed from Raymond Brown the idea that Mary is the spokesperson of the *anawim.*

Chapter ten, "God's Reign on Earth," draws chiefly from:

Viviano, Benedict. *The Kingdom of God in History.* Wilmington: Glazier, 1988.

The treatment on *shalom* in chapter thirteen, "The Meek," relies on:

Leon-Dufour, Xavier. "Peace." *Dictionary of Biblical Theology.* New York: Seabury, 1977, pp. 411–414.

The chapters on the individual beatitudes were enriched by:

Gelin, Albert. *The Poor of Yahweh*. Collegeville: The Liturgical Press, 1964.

Bernard, P. R. *Le Mystere de Jesus*. Paris: Salvator-Mulhouse, 1961, Tome I, pp. 307–316.

Barth, Gerhard. "Matthew's Understanding of the Law." In Bornkamm, Barth and Held. *Tradition and Interpretation in Matthew*. Philadelphia: Westminster, 1963, pp. 105–136.

General reference:

Harrington, Daniel. *Sacra Pagina: The Gospel of Matthew*. Collegeville: Glazier, 1991.

Zerwick, Max and Mary Grosvenor. *A Grammatical Analysis of the Greek New Testament*. Rome: Biblical Institute Press, 1979.

Abbreviations

Unless otherwise noted, all Scripture quotations are from *The New Revised Standard Version* of the Bible. Other translations are abbreviated as follows:

AUTHOR	Author's translation
KJV	King James Version
MLV	Modern Language Version
NAB	New American Bible
NEB	New English Bible
NJB	New Jerusalem Bible
RSV	Revised Standard Version
SPENCE	Translation by Rev. Francis Aloysius Spence, OP, copyright © 1937 by the Macmillan Co.

Part One

The Spirituality
of the *Anawim*

1

The Holy Remnant

One day Jesus climbed a mountain, sat down and began to teach his disciples. They crowded around him, jostling each other as they strained to hear, wondering how this poor man from Nazareth had gotten his learning. Jesus began by proclaiming what we call the beatitudes, for they show us how to find happiness. His disciples understood his words according to their Israelite mentality, formed by the Scriptures and traditions of their people. Jesus proclaimed the beatitudes in the vocabulary and spirituality of the *anawim,* Yahweh's "poor ones." Israel's rich religious heritage fully flowered in this *anawim* spirituality.

Yahweh's poor ones knew their poverty before God and their utter need of him. From him alone could they receive the salvation promised to them in the hoped-for messianic kingdom. The beatitudes have a messianic meaning. They proclaim that the kingdom of God is at hand, already at work in the messiah who has come. "If it is by the finger of God that I cast out the demons," says Jesus, "then the kingdom of God has come to you" (Lk 11:20). The messiah's presence fulfills the highest desires of Yahweh's poor.

This basic messianic meaning of the beatitudes was later enriched with a deeper understanding of the messianic kingdom as life in the Holy Spirit. After Pentecost, in the light of the Holy Spirit, the Church saw that the beatitudes can be lived in their fullness only under the influence of the Holy Spirit, who is the messianic gift par excellence. Hence the beautiful work done by St. Augustine and St. Thomas Aquinas showing the connection of the beatitudes with the virtues and graces of the Holy Spirit.

This book will be concerned primarily with the messianic meaning of the beatitudes as presented in the concepts and vocabulary of the *anawim,* Yahweh's poor ones.

Who, then, are the *anawim,* and what is their spirituality? The *anawim* are called Yahweh's poor ones because Yahweh fashioned them for himself as a holy remnant taken from among his people Israel. This holy remnant would be the true Israel, and through it, God would carry out his purposes of salvation.

The prophets saw the trials that befell Israel as God's purifying action upon his people that would leave a remnant like the stump of a felled tree. "Even if a tenth part remain in it, it will be burned again, like a terebinth or an oak whose stump remains standing when it is felled. The holy seed is its stump" (Is 6:13). Like a seed pushing through soil, the remnant, the stump, would spring into new and holy life.

The kingdom of the future, the holy remnant, grows from the stump that remains from the felling of the present kingdom.

> On that day the remnant of Israel and the survivors of the house of Jacob will no more lean on the one who struck them [Assyria], but will lean on the Lord, the Holy One of Israel, in truth. A remnant will return, the remnant of Jacob, to the mighty God. For though your people Israel were like the sand of the sea, only a remnant of them will return (Is 10:20–22).

The prophet Zephaniah gave the holy remnant their name, the *anawim,* "the poor ones." Exhorting the people to poverty of spirit, he says, "Seek the Lord, all you humble *(anawim)* of the land, who do his commands; seek righteousness, seek humility *(anawah);* perhaps you may be hidden on the day of the Lord's wrath" (Zeph 2:3). Righteousness and humility will characterize Yahweh's poor, the holy remnant.

Zephaniah goes on to say how Yahweh will purify his people, leaving them humble and lowly:

> On that day you shall not be put to shame because of all the deeds by which you have rebelled against me, for then I will remove from your midst your proudly exultant ones, and you shall no longer be haughty in my holy mountain. For I will leave in the midst of you *a people humble and lowly.* They shall seek refuge in the name of the Lord—*the remnant of Israel;* they shall do no wrong and utter no lies, nor shall a deceitful tongue be found in their mouths. Then they will pasture and lie down, and no one shall make them afraid (Zeph 3:11–13).

Zephaniah was not the first prophet to speak about the remnant. Long before him, Amos had spoken of the holy remnant: "Hate evil and love good, and establish justice in the gate; it may be that the Lord, the God of hosts, will be gracious to the remnant of Joseph" (Amos 5:15).

The prophet Isaiah had such a strong faith in God's promise to purify a holy remnant that he gave his son a symbolic name: "Shear-jashub—a remnant shall return" (cf. Is 7:3; 10:22). God would accomplish his will to form a holy remnant. Even if some of his people prove unfaithful, the Lord remains forever faithful to his covenant with Israel. Through the faithful remnant, God will fulfill his covenant promises.

To belong to the remnant and be saved, one must be righteous, that is, just in all one's dealings, so that justice will prevail. The righteous person strives to do what is right in every situation. For covenant people, the covenant indicates the right thing to do. Righteousness and fidelity to the covenant are two aspects of the same thing. Therefore, Isaiah calls redeemed Jerusalem "the city of righteousness, the faithful city" (Is 1:26).

When everyone does righteousness *(ṣedeq)*—the right thing in each situation—justice *(mishpat)* results among the people. Yahweh himself by his purifying action brings about this condition of redeemed righteousness and justice in his people. In his dealings with them, God's righteousness is fidelity to his covenant with them. Justice and righteousness shall characterize the remnant when God has purified them. As a people cleansed of its evils, the restored remnant will be holy:

> Whoever is left in Zion and remains in Jerusalem will be called holy, everyone who has been recorded for life in Jerusalem, once the Lord has washed away the filth of the daughters of Zion and cleansed the bloodstains of Jerusalem from its midst by a spirit of judgment and by a spirit of burning (Is 4:3–4).

A Messianic People

According to Isaiah, the messiah will spring from the holy remnant.

> A shoot shall come out from the stump of Jesse, and a branch shall grow out of its roots. The spirit of the Lord shall rest on him.... With righteousness he shall judge the poor, and decide with equity for the meek of the earth.... Righteousness shall be the belt around his waist, and faithfulness the belt around his loins (Is 11:1–5).

Thus the messiah, the shoot from the stump, the holy seed, will establish the poor and lowly remnant in fidelity and righteousness. God's people shall then "be called the city of righteousness, the faithful city" (Is 1:26).

When at last the messiah comes, the *anawim*, Yahweh's poor ones, will receive him. Their hearts have been prepared by prophets such as Isaiah, Amos, Jeremiah, Zephaniah, whom God used to form for himself "a people humble and lowly...they shall seek refuge in the name of the Lord—the remnant of Israel" (Zeph 3:12). Though the prophets began this work of God, God himself brought it to perfection, drawing good even out of severe sufferings such as the Assyrian invasion and the Babylonian exile. The remnant grows among the exiles. In exile they return to the Lord, purified by their sufferings.

After the return from exile, the prophet Zechariah declares that the holy remnant needs further purification before it can be called the people of God, the true Israel:

> In the whole land, says the Lord, two thirds shall be cut off and perish, and one third shall be left alive. And I will put this third into the fire, refine them as one refines silver, and test them as gold is tested. They will call on my name, and I will answer them. I will say, "They are my people"; and they will say, "The Lord is our God" (Zech 13:8–9).

Only the purified, holy remnant, the poor ones, deserve the title, "God's People."

The purity of heart necessary for seeing God does not come easily. We need to be refined like gold and silver in the fire. God does not want us to suffer; he does not directly cause evil. But he can draw good out of evil. Only in such trials do we arrive at the poverty of spirit needed for receiving the kingdom.

In proclaiming the beatitudes to his disciples, using the vocabulary of the *anawim*, Jesus is declaring that those who live these beatitudes belong to the holy remnant that the prophets foretold. "At the present time," says St. Paul, "there is a remnant, chosen by grace" (Rm 11:5). Paul says that we non-Jewish Christians have been grafted into that remnant, like branches into a vinestock. He warns about the danger that we can once again be broken off the vine, and thus cut off from the holy remnant (cf. Rm 11).

We see then how the symbolic name of Isaiah's son, "a remnant shall return," both comforts and warns us. As faithful Christians we have been grafted into the holy remnant, but if we fall from faith and faithfulness, we shall be cut off again. Will we still belong to the holy remnant when God in our times has finished purifying his Church? Or will we fall away? It depends on how we live the beatitudes.

2

The *Anawim* in the Psalms

The holy remnant that God formed fully deserved the title, "God's people" (Zech 13:8–9). They had remained faithful to the covenant. As the *anawim,* they are "a people poor and lowly," humble of heart, trusting in the Lord alone. Thus *"anawim"* became almost synonymous with "God's people": "For the Lord takes pleasure in his people; he adorns the humble *(anawim)* with victory" (Ps 149:4). This is typical Hebrew parallelism: a statement is made, then repeated in equivalent words. "His people" and "the humble" express the same thing. The *anawim* are the true Israel.

The characteristics of the *anawim* form an ideal for the people of God. They are fully God's people in the sense that they entrust themselves totally to him to be his own, guided by his wisdom, protected by his power, nourished by his love. This does not mean that those who fall short of this ideal have been rejected from God's people. As St. Paul says so emphatically, "the gifts and the calling of God are irrevocable" (Rm 11:29). But the *anawim* open themselves more fully to the Lord's blessings, and so Jesus declares them blessed: "Blessed are the poor in spirit, for theirs is the kingdom of heaven" (Mt 5:3).

The faithful remnant were the humble of heart, purified of pride and complacency through suffering, and trusting now in God alone: "Sing for joy, O heavens, and exult, O earth; break forth, O mountains, into singing! For the Lord has comforted his people, and will have compassion on his suffering ones *(aniyyim)*" (Is 49:13).

In their sufferings, the *aniyyim* had become *anawim,* humble and poor. *Aniyyim* and *anawim* mean practically the same thing—poor, afflicted, lowly, humble, meek. *Aniyyim,* however, emphasizes the objective poverty and afflictions that brought the people low, while *anawim* emphasizes the subjective attitude of humility and poverty of spirit learned in these sufferings. The messiah has been sent to these poor ones: "He has sent me to bring good news to the oppressed *(anawim),* to bind up the brokenhearted...to comfort all who mourn" (Is 61:1–2).

In expressing the beatitudes, the foundations of the Christian life, in the vocabulary of the *anawim,* Jesus declares that *anawim* spirituality is intrinsic to Christian spirituality. Poverty of spirit, meekness, mourning, hunger and thirst for righteousness, mercy, purity of heart, peacemaking, suffering persecution—as we shall see from the prophets and psalms of Israel—all characterize the *anawim,* and Jesus requires them of his followers. Christian living calls for all these qualities of the *anawim.* The spirituality of the humble and lowly lies in openness and receptivity to Jesus' work as messiah, the Giver of all the blessings of salvation.

St. Luke presents Mary, the Mother of the Lord, as one of the *anawim.* She enjoys all beatitude: "Blessed is she who believed that there would be a fulfillment of what was spoken to her by the Lord" (Lk 1:45). In her Magnificat, Mary speaks for the *anawim,* using their vocabulary. Every verse in the Magnificat echoes a verse in the psalms, which clearly express the qualities of the *anawim.* By putting Mary before our eyes as the model of all believers, St. Luke canonizes *anawim* spirituality. Those who pray the psalms will grow in this spirituality, and therefore in the beatitudes. Praying the Church's Liturgy of the Hours, which uses all of the psalms, will form us in this spirituality. So too will an attentive praying of the responsorial psalms in the Liturgy of the Word at Mass.

Psalm 34

Psalm 34 describes the characteristics of the *anawim* in an especially rich way. The psalmist invites all the poor to praise and thank God with him: "I will bless the Lord at all times; his praise shall be continually in my mouth. My soul makes its boast in the Lord; let the humble *(aniyyim)* hear and be glad. O magnify the Lord with me, and let us exalt his name together" (Ps 34:1–3).

God had made a covenant with his people. Therefore the *anawim*, God's faithful remnant, had a strong sense of community support. The psalmist expresses this community spirit when he appeals to the faithful to join him in thanking God. He calls the people to rejoice with him because God has blessed him. No doubt he had previously called upon the community to support him and pray for him in his distress: "I sought the Lord and he answered me, and delivered me from all my fears" (v. 4). Now he wants the community to praise and thank God with him: "Look to him and be radiant; so your faces shall never be ashamed. This poor soul cried, and was heard by the Lord, and was saved from every trouble" (vv. 5–6). Not only should they rejoice with him; what the Lord has done for him should inspire them, too, to look to Yahweh and confidently expect help in time of need.

The psalmist continues, listing various qualities of the poor ones. They take refuge in the Lord, and as his holy ones, they fear him: "O taste and see that the Lord is good; happy are those who take refuge in him. O fear the Lord, you his holy ones, for those who fear him have no want" (vv. 8–9). Fear of the Lord means reverent submission to him.

They seek the Lord: "Those who seek the Lord lack no

good thing" (v. 10). They tell the truth and do no evil: "Keep your tongue from evil, and your lips from speaking deceit. Depart from evil, and do good" (vv. 13–14). Free from the evildoing and deceit that destroy peace, they make peace: "Seek peace and pursue it" (v. 14).

Thus they act as Zephaniah stated the holy remnant would act: "For I will leave in the midst of you a people humble and lowly. They shall seek refuge in the name of the Lord—the remnant of Israel. They shall do no wrong and utter no lies, nor shall a deceitful tongue be found in their mouths" (Zeph 3:12–13).

Perhaps these words of Zephaniah inspired Psalm 34. The psalmist was exhorting the people to live the ideal the prophet had placed before them, and so cooperate with the Lord in forming the true Israel, the poor and lowly ones.

The psalm calls the poor ones the "righteous": "The eyes of the Lord are on the righteous, and his ears are open to their cry.... When the righteous cry for help, the Lord hears, and rescues them from all their troubles" (vv. 15–17).

Righteousness means fidelity to the religious, moral and social requirements of the covenant. "Righteousness" and "faithfulness" become two words for the same thing: "Afterward you shall be called the city of righteousness, the faithful city" (Is 1:26). The righteous deserved the title God's People: "Your people shall all be righteous; they shall possess the land forever" (Is 60:21). "They shall be called, 'the Holy People, the Redeemed of the Lord'" (Is 62:12).

They are the brokenhearted, who truly repent their sins: "The Lord is near to the brokenhearted, and saves the crushed in spirit" (v. 18). This brokenheartedness springs from sorrow for sin, not merely the dejection resulting from a hard lot in life. Another psalm speaks of this repentance: "Let the bones that you have crushed rejoice. Hide your face from my sins, and blot out all my iniquities. Create in me a clean heart, and put a new and right spirit within me" (Ps 51:8–10). The messiah will comfort these mourners: "He has sent me to bring good news to the oppressed, to bind up the brokenhearted...to comfort all who mourn" (Is 61:1–2). "Blessed are those who mourn, for they will be comforted" (Mt 5:4).

Likewise, the *anawim* are called the Lord's servants: "The Lord redeems the life of his servants; none of those who take refuge in him will be condemned" (Ps 34:22).

Psalm 37

Psalm 37 expresses other aspects of the spirituality of the *anawim*. Yahweh's poor ones wait for him in patience. Their hope and trust never waver even when they have to wait a long time for God to act. Indeed, to wait upon the Lord means to hope in him: "Be still before the Lord, and wait patiently for him.... Those who wait for the Lord shall inherit the land" (Ps 37:7, 9). This patient hope in the Lord reflects humble meekness: "Trust in the Lord, and do good; so you will live in the land, and enjoy security" (v. 3). "The meek *(anawim)* shall inherit the land" (v. 11).

Yahweh's poor suffer persecution: "The wicked draw the sword and bend their bows to bring down the poor and needy, to kill those who walk uprightly" (v. 14). The wicked oppose them because of their righteousness. "But the Lord upholds the righteous" (v. 17).

"The righteous are generous and keep giving" (v. 21). They show mercy to the needy. As Yahweh's poor ones, they enjoy the Lord's blessing: "Those blessed by the Lord shall inherit the land" (v. 22). "The righteous shall inherit the land, and live in it forever" (v. 29). "Wait for the Lord, and keep to his way, and he will exalt you to inherit the land.... The salvation of the righteous is from the Lord; he is their refuge in the time of trouble" (vv. 34, 39).

Yahweh's poor are faithful: "He will not forsake his

faithful ones" (v. 28). They are wholehearted, totally given to the Lord: "The Lord watches over the lives of the wholehearted; their inheritance lasts forever" (v. 18 NAB). "Watch the wholehearted one, and mark the upright" (v. 37 NAB). The word translated as "wholehearted" *(tamim)* is often translated as "blameless." But its root meaning is "whole, entire, complete." A human person is whole, completely integrated, blameless, only when he or she is wholeheartedly devoted to the Lord.

Yahweh's poor live in peace and make peace: "There is posterity for the peaceable" (v. 37).

Despite these remarkable promises, God's people often found that the wicked prosper while the just suffer. For Christians, this problem of suffering finds its solution only in Jesus, who alone satisfies our hunger and thirst for justice, and gives the kingdom to the persecuted.

More than ten times the psalms use the expression, "I am poor and needy," which is the basic confession of the *anawim:* (Ps 35:10; 37:14; 40:17; 69:29; 70:5; 72:4; 74:21; 82:3; 86:1; 109:16, 22):

> O Lord, make haste to help me!
> Let those be put to shame and confusion
>   who seek my life....
> Let all who seek you
>   rejoice and be glad in you.
> Let those who love your salvation
>   say evermore, "God is great!"
> But I am poor and needy;
>   hasten to me, O God!
> You are my help and deliverer;
> O Lord, do not delay! (Ps 70:1–2, 4–5).

All this provides a necessary background for understanding the first beatitude, "Blessed are the poor in spirit." Indeed, this beatitude sums up all the others. Zephaniah describes the holy remnant as "a people humble and lowly" who "seek refuge in the name of the Lord." They are blessed because they hope in the Lord.

In the psalms we find the rich vocabulary that Jesus will use in proclaiming the beatitudes. As the poor One par excellence, Jesus will pour into these words and concepts a new wealth of meaning.

3

"The Proud" Versus "the Poor"

The *anawim,* Yahweh's humble and lowly ones, can be best understood in contrast with their opposites, the proud, who oppress the poor. The Lord refers to this contrast when he says through the prophet Zephaniah, "I will remove from your midst the proudly exultant ones, and you will no longer be haughty on my holy mountain, for I will leave in the midst of you a people humble and lowly" (Zeph 3:11–12). "The proud" are the opposite of "the poor," who take refuge in Yahweh.

The psalms repeatedly contrast the proud and the humble, the wicked and the righteous. The first psalm announces this theme, which constantly recurs in the psalter. It contrasts the two ways—the way of the righteous and the way of the wicked. "Happy are those who do not follow the advice of the wicked, or take the path that sinners tread, or sit in the seat of scoffers; but their delight is the law of the Lord, and on his law they meditate day and night" (Ps 1:1–2).

The wicked will come to nothing, "like chaff that the wind drives away" (v. 4), but the righteous will "yield their fruit in its season" (v. 3). "For the Lord watches over the way of the righteous, but the way of the wicked will perish" (v. 6). Again and again in the psalms, the righteous refer to themselves as "the poor."

Psalm 2

Psalm 2 further contrasts the wicked and the righteous, and more clearly defines the *anawim*. In this psalm, the wicked "set themselves...against the Lord and his anointed" and conspire to "burst their bonds asunder" (2:2–3). The bonds they reject are the Lord's law. Far from conspiring against the Lord and rejecting his law, the righteous "delight...in the law of the Lord" (1:2), directing their life and activities by it. The word "law" translates the Hebrew word *torah,* which means "instruction." It derives from a root word meaning "to point the way." By his *torah,* the Lord shows the way.

The *anawim,* who "delight...in the law of the Lord," willingly humble themselves before the divine majesty and accept his ways, while the wicked conspire to throw off his yoke (cf. Ps 2:1–3). The words *anawim* and *aniyyim* derive from a primitive root meaning "abased, depressed, bowed down," and the name *anawim* literally means "bent low." The *anawim* willingly bow down to the Lord and submit to his ways, while the wicked rebel. This contrast between the proud and the humble more clearly defines the *anawim,* who willingly surrender to the Lord.

The psalm says that the Lord's anointed, the king he sets up on Mt. Zion, will break the rebellious "with a rod of iron" (2:9). The psalmist warns: "Serve the Lord with fear, with trembling kiss his feet" (2:11). The psalm ends by declaring, "Happy are all who take refuge in him" (2:12).

Thus the first psalm begins with a beatitude, "Happy are those who do not follow the advice of the wicked" (1:1), and the second psalm ends with one: "Happy are all who take refuge in him" (2:12). Since the whole psalter repeatedly contrasts the wicked and the righteous, the proud and the poor, we can say that the psalter proclaims beatitude. Happy are those whose "delight is in the law of the Lord" (1:2), "who take refuge in him" (2:12). Other explicit beatitudes occur in the psalms, such as, "Happy are those who fear the Lord, who greatly delight in his commandments" (Ps 112:1); "Happy are the people to whom such blessings fall; happy are the people whose God is the Lord" (144:15); "Happy are those whose help is the God of Jacob, whose hope is in the Lord their God" (146:5).

Repeatedly in the psalms, the poor and lowly righteous, who suffer oppression, take refuge in the Lord. "Many are rising against me...but you O Lord are a shield around me, my glory, and the one who lifts up my head" (3:1, 3). "I lie down and sleep; I wake again, for the Lord sustains me" (3:5). "I will both lie down and sleep in peace; for you alone, O Lord, make me lie down in safety" (4:8).

The first two psalms announce the victor in the great battle between the wicked and the righteous. "The way of the wicked will perish" (1:6). The victory will belong to the *anawim*, who have humbly bowed down to the Lord and submitted to his ways. In imagery like that of Psalm 2, psalm 149 announces that the *anawim* will act as God's instrument in overcoming evil:

> For the Lord takes pleasure in his people;
>   he *adorns the humble* with victory...
> Let the high praises of God be in their throats
>   and two-edged swords in their hands
> to execute vengeance on the nations
>   and punishment on the peoples,
> to bind their kings with fetters
>   and their nobles with fetters of iron
> to execute on them the judgment decreed.
>   This is glory for all his faithful ones.
> Praise the Lord! (149:4–9).

To trace through the psalter this contrast between the righteous and the wicked, the poor and the proud, can be a fascinating study. It sums up all human history as a cosmic

battle pitting the proud against God and his anointed one.
In the second psalm, which sets the theme for the entire
psalter, "the nations conspire," "the peoples plot," their
rulers "set themselves...against the Lord and his anointed."
It does not simply concern individuals; whole nations oppress God's chosen people. Psalm 9 also describes the
anawim as "the oppressed," "the afflicted," "those who
know your name," who "put their trust in you," "who seek
you." Their adversaries are "the nations."

> You have rebuked the nations,
>   you have destroyed the wicked...
>   the very memory of them has perished.
> But the Lord sits enthroned forever,
>   he has established his throne for judgment.
> He judges the world with righteousness;
>   he judges the peoples with equity.
> The Lord is a stronghold for the oppressed,
>   a stronghold in time of trouble,
> And those who know your name put their trust
>   in you,
>   for you, O Lord, have not forsaken those who
>   seek you....
> He does not forget the cry of the afflicted
>   (Ps 9:5–12).

The first Christians interpreted the persecution against
them in the light of Psalm 2. When Peter and John were
arrested after curing the crippled beggar, the authorities
commanded them to stop preaching the name of Jesus and
dismissed them with threats. They came home to the community and reported what had happened. The whole community understood what was going on, saying,

> Sovereign Lord, who made the heaven and the earth,
> the sea and everything in them, it is you who said by
> the Holy Spirit through our ancestor David, your
> servant, "Why did the Gentiles rage, and the peoples

imagine vain things? The kings of the earth took their stand, and the rulers have gathered together against the Lord and against his messiah." For in this city, in fact, both Herod and Pontius Pilate... gathered together against your holy servant Jesus, whom you anointed... (Acts 4:24–27).

This interpretation of Psalm 2 by the first Christian community, who saw it being fulfilled in Jesus Christ and his followers, prepares the way for a Christological interpretation of the psalter. This psalm at the beginning sets the theme of all the psalms. When this psalm is seen as fulfilled in Jesus, as the Acts of the Apostles presents it, we see his involvement in the whole struggle as presented in all the psalms.

In summary, the psalter dramatizes the struggle between the two ways, the way of the wicked and the way of the righteous. Psalm 149 tells of the final outcome of the battle, and Psalm 150 praises Yahweh for his marvelous deeds in winning the victory. In praying psalm 150 in the light of Christ, we praise God for his salvific deeds accomplished in the death and resurrection of Jesus, his anointed servant, the one against whom the nations and kings raged, but could not prevail.

The great antithesis in the psalms, the righteous versus the sinners, the poor versus the proud, foreshadows the challenge of Jesus: Are you for me, or are you against me? "Whoever is not with me is against me!" (Mt 12:30). We cannot compromise with evil. We must decide for the Lord and for Jesus, his anointed One. Jesus' followers must expect to suffer persecution for righteousness' sake. God's poor and lowly ones, oppressed by the proud, will hunger and thirst for righteousness, desiring that the Lord vindicate the oppressed and establish justice. Thus the great struggle between the wicked and the righteous as the psalter presents it provides important background for understanding the beatitudes.

The Power of Praise and Intercession

Just as the first Christians got fully involved in the great struggle between good and evil, Christians today need to work for the good. One important way to do this is to pray the psalms in the Liturgy of the Hours. Psalm 149, quoted earlier, shows the righteous winning the victory by the power of praising God and by the power of his word. The glory of Israel will consist in helping Yahweh establish his reign despite the power of evil.

The liturgy of praise plays a key role in the ultimate victory of good over evil. The Church's liturgy is the prayer of the whole People of God, and the Church prays only in union with Christ her Head. The Lord Jesus himself praises God the Father through the praises his people offer. Such praise has inestimable power to win the victory. It parallels and complements the power of the inspired Word of God that goes forth from the Lord's mouth: "From his mouth comes a sharp sword with which to strike down the nations, and he will rule them with a rod of iron" (Rev 19:15).

Isaiah beautifully expresses the role of intercession in bringing about salvation and the vindication of God's oppressed people:

> For Zion's sake I will not keep silent,
> and for Jerusalem's sake I will not rest,
> until her vindication shines out like the dawn,
> and her salvation like a burning torch (Is 62:1).

Why will the prophet not keep silent and why will he take no rest? For two reasons. He must repeatedly proclaim Yahweh's promise of salvation, lest the people lose hope when God delays fulfilling the promise. And he must continue to cry out to Yahweh, asking him to speed up the fulfillment. Isaiah calls upon the city's watchmen to join him in this intercession, to give Yahweh no rest, but to cry out to him incessantly till he hears their prayers:

Upon your walls, O Jerusalem,
  I have posted sentinels;
all day and night
  they shall never be silent.
You who remind the Lord,
  take no rest,
and give him no rest
  until he establishes Jerusalem
  and makes it renowned throughout the earth
    (Is 62:6–7).

The sentinels bear a great responsibility, for through their unwearying intercession they hasten the Lord's victory over evil. All who pray the Church's Liturgy of the Hours also share this responsibility. Their glory is to share in this victory, to hasten its coming.

Just as the wicked gather together to oppose the Lord, so the righteous gather together into the community of God's people. The *anawim* had a deep sense of community solidarity. As a people they advanced the Lord's cause. They loved the assembly: "I will give thanks to the Lord with my whole heart, in the company of the upright, in the congregation" (Ps 111:1). They confided in each other, praised and thanked God together, appealed to one another for support, and reminded the Lord of his promises. "How very good and pleasant it is when kindred live together in unity!" (Ps 133:1). "Come, bless the Lord, all you servants of the Lord, who stand by night in the house of the Lord! Lift up your hands to the holy place, and bless the Lord" (Ps 134:1–2).

4

The Poor One Par Excellence

Psalm 22

Who in the Hebrew Scriptures best shows forth all the qualities of Yahweh's poor ones, the *anawim?* It is the one who cries out in Psalm 22, "My God, my God, why have you forsaken me." He calls himself poor and afflicted: "You who fear the Lord, praise him.... For he did not despise or abhor the affliction of the afflicted" (vv. 23–24).

He is the poor one *par excellence* not because of the severity of his trials, but because of his *attitude* in these afflictions, the way he bears them. Sufferings crush him, yet he endures them in trusting acceptance, in peaceful abandonment to Yahweh.

He expresses no rebellion against his hard lot, no resentment toward God, no bitterness toward his oppressors and persecutors. He shows meekness, in the strong sense of the beatitude, "Blessed are the meek." Although God seems to have abandoned him—"Why are you so far from helping me, from the words of my groaning" (v. 1)—he enjoys peace, for deep in his heart he knows in faith that God supports him. Had he given up all hope of God hearing him, he would not have continued to cry to him.

He has reason to keep on trusting. In addressing the psalm to "My God," he uses covenant terminology. "My God" echoes the great covenant formula the Lord used, "I will be their God, and they shall be my people" (Jer 31:33).

Addressing his lament to the God of the covenant implies faith that the Lord will be faithful to his covenant, and can be trusted to help his afflicted one. To call him "my God" already shows trust, no matter how desperate the complaint, no matter how deep the anguish and seeming despair it springs from.

The psalmist's God is the God of the covenant, who has always stayed close to his people. God rules as their king, acclaimed with praise: "You are holy, enthroned on the praises of Israel" (v. 3). "In you our ancestors trusted; they trusted, and you delivered them.... In you they trusted, and were not put to shame" (vv. 4–5). Because God upheld his covenant with them, he will uphold his covenant with the psalmist. For God made the same covenant with them and with him.

"It was you who took me from the womb; you kept me safe on my mother's breast. On you I was cast from my birth, and since my mother bore me you have been my God" (vv. 9–10). Just as the psalmist rested in his mother's arms as a child, even now he trusts the One who has been his God since his birth, whom he still calls "my God" (vv. 1, 2, 10).

If he trusts God so strongly, why does he lament so much? He cries out in pain, listing all his sufferings, because they cause him such intense distress, so deeply experienced, that he cannot restrain his cries. How could he not cry out in pain? "Many bulls encircle me, strong bulls of Bashan surround me; they open wide their mouths at me, like a ravening and roaring lion. I am poured out like water, and all my bones are out of joint; my heart is like wax; it is melted within my breast; my mouth is dried up like a potsherd, and my tongue sticks to my jaws; you lay me in the dust of death..." (vv. 12–15).

Yet he lists his afflictions without resentment or rebellion, not hating his persecutors. He refers to them as "strong bulls, ravening lions, dogs, wild oxen." He uses this powerful imagery, not because he hates his persecutors, but to describe the fury and viciousness of their oppression.

By listing his troubles he cries out in trust to God, his only hope: "Do not be far from me, for trouble is near and there is no one to help" (v. 11)—no one but God! His trust in God stands out all the more because his persecutors mock him on account of this trust: "All who see me mock at me; they make mouths at me, they shake their heads; 'Commit your cause to the Lord; let him deliver—let him rescue the one in whom he delights'" (vv. 7–8). The psalmist renews his lifelong trust in the Lord who has been his God since his birth: "Since my mother bore me you have been my God" (v. 10). He continues to trust: "Do not be far from me, for trouble is near" (v. 11).

No doubt the psalmist's peaceful trust in God resulted from a long learning experience. If he can now peacefully bear such persecution and oppression without resentment or hatred, he has probably gone through a crucible of hardships and difficulties. He has learned to trust in the Lord by experiencing human poverty and neediness before God.

The psalmist uses much of the same imagery as Jeremiah. Possibly he has learned from Jeremiah's lamentation, meditating upon that prophet's long struggle to accept suffering for the Lord in peaceful trust. His psalm probably bore the fruit of an ongoing struggle. No doubt it summarizes a long experience of persecution, in which he came only gradually to this attitude of trusting acceptance. His peaceful abandonment of self to God could not have come easily.

From Lamentation to Praise

The psalmist's long, anguished lament suddenly turns into a hymn of praise: "Save me from the mouth of the lion.... You who fear the Lord, praise him!" (vv. 21–23). Why this sudden transition from lament to praise?

The psalm was probably composed for a *todah,* a thanksgiving liturgy. In a *todah,* the person thanking God would invite his friends to a thanksgiving sacrifice. The assembly would offer an animal to God and then eat it in a festive meal. The person giving thanks would state his reasons for praising and thanking God, and invite his guests to join him in thanksgiving and praise.

So that the praise and thanks would be all the more heartfelt, the author of this psalm recounts in detail all the horrors his persecutors have inflicted on him. This explains why he uses such powerful imagery. He dramatizes his sufferings poetically as though these afflictions still torment him: "My God, my God, why have you forsaken me? Why are you so far from helping me, from the words of my groaning? O my God, I cry by day, but you do not answer; and by night, but find no rest" (vv. 1–2).

But he ends his litany of suffering by crying, "You have answered me!" (v. 21). This is a more exact translation of the original Hebrew than the Greek version of the Bible has. The Greek translates it as "Save my lowliness" or "Save my poor life." The Hebrew word for "poor, lowly," is *ani,* while the Hebrew for "answer" is *anah.* The translators into Greek may have confused these two similar words, perhaps because of a faulty manuscript.

The Greek translation, "Save my poor life / my lowliness" has influenced many modern translations. Since this psalm voices the cry of a poor one, the Greek version fits in with the theme of the psalm. But "You have answered me," or "you have rescued me," seems to be a preferable translation, for it corresponds to the opening cry of the psalm, "You do not answer" (v. 1). We often experience this when God seems so slow to answer our prayers. Yet sooner or later, if we continue to trust, we can say with joy and praise, "You have answered me!"

The words, "You do not answer" (v. 1) and "You have

answered me" (v. 21) frame the psalm's long list of afflictions. This highlights the psalm's meaning: no matter how much we suffer, God will answer our trusting cry; be ready to praise and thank him. This emphasizes the psalmist's point that God does hear our prayers.

The psalmist ends his litany of suffering by crying out, "You have answered me!" He promises that he will proclaim what the Lord has done for him and glorify God: "I will tell of your name to my brothers and sisters; in the midst of the congregation I will praise you: You who fear the Lord, praise him! All you offspring of Jacob, glorify him; stand in awe of him, all you offspring of Israel! For he did not despise or abhor the affliction of the afflicted; he did not hide his face from me, *but heard when I cried to him.* From you comes my praise in the great congregation" (vv. 22–25). The psalmist invites the whole assembly to praise God with him, for God has answered his prayer.

In this we see another trait of Yahweh's poor ones: their strong community spirit as God's people. They find mutual support in their troubles, and together they thank and praise God.

The Cry of Jesus

Psalm 22, an afflicted one's lament, praise and thanks, became the common property of all Israel. It voices the universal cry of the human heart suffering before God. Adopted into the psalter, it belonged also to Jesus of Nazareth, who regularly prayed with his fellow Jews in the synagogues. As a poor and afflicted one, despised by those who rejected his preaching, Jesus no doubt prayed this psalm often to deepen his trust in his heavenly Father and to sustain him in his suffering. It sprang spontaneously from his heart to his lips as he hung crucified, to express his interior prayer as he agonized on the cross.

Thus he identifies with the agony and faith of countless

generations of *anawim,* afflicted and persecuted people. He unites himself with all who suffer, and lifts them all to the Father in trusting prayer. Praying this psalm on the cross, Jesus reveals his suffering heart. He suffers in every suffering person, who will all join him in praising God once he has answered their prayers.

The risen Christ appeals to us in our afflictions to trust the Father just as he did. He could say: "When it seems that God has forsaken you, trust anyway. He will answer. Abandon yourself completely to him, as I did on the cross: 'Father, into your hands I commend my spirit' (Lk 23:46)."

What This Psalm Means for Us

Jesus made this psalm his own, just as the covenant people before him had made it their own. It expressed beautifully the depths of their misery and the strength of their trust in God. But when Jesus made it his own, he gave it a new richness of meaning. When we pray it now, we can think of Jesus praying it with us and in us, crying out in our cries, forming in us his own trust in the Father. We too make this psalm our own, praying it in union with Jesus.

As we pray this psalm, we hear Jesus on the cross praying it. We hear him crying out these words of anguish in the voices of all who suffer today. He has taken up into his own suffering the cries of all the afflicted ones of all time: victims of violence and war, abandoned children, the sick and suffering, the homeless, the addicted, the poor. His cry echoes in everyone's cry; everyone's cry echoes in his cry on the cross.

We offer to the Father in heaven this voice of the crucified Jesus as it rises from the hearts of all the afflicted, but especially from our loved ones. In the cry of Jesus we offer also our personal cries of suffering.

The cry of Jesus to the Father as he hung on the cross rose also from the Immaculate Heart of Mary. As she stood by the cross looking at her dying son, in her heart she offered Jesus' cry to the Father. As this cry of Jesus rises from suffering hearts everywhere, we offer it to the Father in the heart of Mary, our Mother.

Trusting in the Father's infinite mercy, we will declare "And he answered me!" God will hear us just as he heard Jesus' cry on the cross. Then we will join the risen Jesus in giving thanks in the Eucharistic assembly. With him we give thanks already for the blessings God will bestow on us through the sacrifice of Jesus. In the Eucharist the risen Lord gives thanks for all the fruits of his sacrifice on the cross, and we offer his praise and thanksgiving as our own.

As we pray Psalm 22 in union with Christ, in the last part (vv. 25–31) we hear him proclaiming the fruits of his sacrifice and praising God for them. He made our poverty and afflictions his own as he hung on the cross. Now we join him in praising and thanking the Father for raising Jesus from death, and raising us up with him. Jesus appeals to the poor, the *anawim* of all times, to join him in praise: "The poor shall eat and be satisfied; those who seek him shall praise the Lord. May your hearts live forever" (v. 26).

When God heard his prayer, the psalmist called upon the whole community to join him in a thanksgiving sacrifice to praise and thank God. Similarly, we can hear the risen Jesus proclaiming in the Christian thanksgiving sacrifice, the Eucharist, that the Father has heard his prayer on the cross. We hear him asking the assembly to praise and thank God with him, for in his prayer, their prayers too are heard: "In the midst of the congregation I will praise you: You who fear the Lord, praise him!" (vv. 22–23). We respond to this invitation, saying, "Through him, with him, in him, in the unity of the Holy Spirit, all glory and honor is yours, almighty Father, forever and ever. Amen."

As we eat the Lord's body and drink his blood in the Eucharist, he fills us with all the blessings of his sacrifice on the cross. "The poor shall eat and be satisfied" (v. 26). The risen Lord says to us, as he nourishes us, "May your hearts live forever!" (v. 26). We praise the Father with him.

God has answered on behalf of all humanity the Lord's cry on the cross, "My God, my God, why have you forsaken me." The fruit of our Lord's sacrifice will draw all people to God: "All the ends of the earth shall remember and turn to the Lord; and all the families of the nations shall worship before him. For dominion belongs to the Lord, and he rules over the nations" (vv. 27–28).

Even the dead will praise God because they will share in the Lord's resurrection. "To him, indeed, shall all who sleep in the earth bow down; before him shall bow all who go down to the dust, and I shall live for him" (v. 29). Acclaiming the crucified Jesus as Lord, the dead shall rise with him and live forever, glorifying God with him in heaven.

All generations till the end of time will join in this song of praise and thanksgiving, for all have been redeemed in the blood of the Lamb: "Posterity will serve him; future generations will be told about the Lord, and proclaim his deliverance to a people yet unborn, saying that he has done it" (vv. 30–31). This unceasing proclamation continues till the end of time in the Christian Eucharistic assembly, and one generation after another joins in the Lord's hymn of praise.

Psalm 116, a typical *todah,* helps form the *anawim* of today in the sentiments they should bring to the Eucharist, our sacrifice of praise and thanksgiving:

> What shall I return to the Lord
>   for all his bounty to me?
> I will lift up the cup of salvation
>   and call on the name of the Lord,
> I will pay my vows to the Lord
>   in the presence of all his people.

Precious in the sight of the Lord
   is the death of his faithful ones.
O Lord, I am your servant;
   I am your servant, the child of your serving girl.
You have loosed my bonds.
I will offer to you a thanksgiving sacrifice
   and call on the name of the Lord.
I will pay my vows to the Lord
   in the presence of all his people (Ps 116:12–18).

PART TWO

THE VIRGIN MARY: SPOKESPERSON OF THE *ANAWIM*

5

The Magnificat: Expression of *Anawim* Spirituality

In Mary, the Mother of Jesus, the spirituality of the *anawim,* Yahweh's poor ones, reaches its full flowering. It radiates in her person and resounds in her song of praise, the Magnificat.

In this song, Mary speaks the language of the *anawim.* Using their vocabulary, she identifies with them. She is their living expression and their spokesperson, especially in thanking God for his help. God responded to their lowliness by sending the messiah, the divine Child whom Mary conceived by the power of the Holy Spirit. In her song, Mary praises God not only for what he has done for her personally in giving her this Child: "The Mighty One has done great things for me" (Lk 1:49). She also sees the conception of her Son as God's gift of mercy to all the *anawim:* "His mercy is for those who fear him from generation to generation" (v. 50).

Mary describes herself in the Magnificat as one of the *anawim* when she says: "My soul magnifies the Lord, and my spirit rejoices in God my Savior, for he has looked with favor on the lowliness of his servant" (Lk 1:46–48).

Scripture usually uses the word "lowliness" to describe the *anawim.* Hannah, Samuel's mother, uses it for her affliction: "O Lord of hosts, if only you will look on the *misery* of your servant, and remember me, and not forget your servant" (1 Sam 1:11).

The same word expresses Mary's "lowliness" and Hannah's "misery": *oni* in Hebrew, *tapeinosis* in Greek. The *anawim* often used this word to describe their needy condition.

In speaking of her lowliness, Mary identifies herself with the "humble and lowly" whom the prophet Zephaniah announced:

> For I will leave in the midst of you
>   a people humble and lowly.
> They shall seek refuge in the name of the Lord—
>   the remnant of Israel (Zeph 3:12–13).

Mary represents this humble and lowly remnant of Israel, in whom the mighty God accomplishes his saving work.

In biblical usage, "lowliness" *(tapeinosis)* had a twofold meaning: "humble state" and "humility." The two ideas are closely related in Hebrew. "Lowliness" is both an objective condition of poverty, neediness or affliction, and a mental attitude—humility.

Like Yahweh's poor ones before her, Mary lives in poverty, one of the powerless in her society. Like the people humble and lowly Zephaniah described, she seeks refuge in the name of the Lord (cf. Zeph 3:13). When she says to the angel Gabriel, "Behold I am the handmaid of the Lord," she expresses not merely her lowliness, but also her humble acceptance of this state. Humble and obedient, she willingly serves God, her Creator and Lord. She trusts herself totally to him and to his loving purposes: "May it be done to me according to your word" (Lk 1:38 NAB).

"He has looked with favor on the lowliness of his servant" (1:48). Looking upon her lowliness and poverty, God who is mighty sees also her humility, her trusting acceptance, and her promptness to serve. Looking upon her openness to him in faith and trust, God responds as Savior with loving favor, pouring out his blessing upon her. Of this Mary sings: "My soul magnifies the Lord, and my spirit rejoices in God my Savior, for he has looked with favor on the lowliness of his servant" (Lk 1:46–48).

In using the vocabulary of the *anawim*, Mary greatly enriches its meaning. In her song, she proclaims that God has fulfilled all the hopes and expectations of the poor ones. He will fulfill them through Mary's virginal conception of her Son, the messiah, which she celebrates in this song. For God responds to the trusting poverty of the *anawim* by sending the messiah.

But this personal presence of God among them as Savior marvelously surpasses all their ardent imaginings and hopes. In singing of the great things the Mighty One has done for her in forming his Son in her womb, Mary clearly shows forth what the *anawim* were looking for as they hungered and thirsted for salvation and hoped in Yahweh.

In her person and in her words, Mary helps us better understand all the traits of the *anawim*. She models these in a perfect way, as an example for us all. These characteristics open the poor and needy to receive the beatitude Mary's Son bestows.

Everything Mary expresses in her humble words in the Magnificat shines forth in her at the annunciation, the visitation, the nativity, the presentation, and all the mysteries she was associated with in Jesus' work of salvation. St. Luke shows Mary as truly Yahweh's poor one, the perfect example of the blessings of the beatitudes. She proclaims this in her song, saying, "Surely, from now on all generations will call me blessed" (1:48).

The word "blessed" finds a place in the vocabulary of the *anawim*. Because the messiah will preach the good news to the poor (cf. Is 61:1), they will be "a people whom the Lord has blessed" (Is 61:9). "Those blessed by the Lord shall inherit the land" (Ps 37:22).

Mary is blessed because her faith and total trust in the Lord have opened her to all the promised blessings. The beatitude Elizabeth addressed to Mary sums up the eight beatitudes: "Blessed is she who believed that there would be a fulfillment of what was spoken to her by the Lord" (1:45). The blessed fruit of her womb fulfills the hopes of Yahweh's poor, those who trusted in the Lord.

St. Luke's Gospel uses the Greek word *makaria* for "blessed," often translated as "happy." But that translation fails to bring out the word's richness in the gospel context, because this happiness concerns a blessing from God, a gift from his love. *Makaria* also points to an eschatological dimension, "signifying that eschatological joy has come" (BROWN, p. 337, note 42).

Makaria had already taken on rich connotations in the biblical tradition, where it denotes being righteous before God. Scripture often expresses being right with God in terms of happiness or blessedness.

Thus we read, "Happy are those who do not follow the advice of the wicked, or take the path that sinners tread... but their delight is in the law of the Lord" (Ps 1:1–2). "Happy are all who take refuge in him" (Ps 2:12). "Happy are those whom you discipline, O Lord, and whom you teach out of your law" (Ps 94:12). "Happy are those who live in your house, ever singing your praise" (Ps 84:4). In these cases, the Greek Bible uses the word *makaria* for "happy," the same word Luke's Gospel uses.

One is truly happy or blessed when he or she is right with God, fully open in faith and trust to receive his blessings. Each of the eight beatitudes expresses a different aspect of this rightness with God which invites and receives his blessings.

Mary's whole person cries out eloquently the words Jesus later spoke, "Blessed rather are those who hear the word of God and obey it" (Lk 11:28). Mary is the perfect disciple, a model for all who hear the word and keep it.

In her Magnificat, she praises God because she, "blessed among women," recipient of all God's blessings in the person of the messiah, is thus herself a blessing for all generations. "All generations will call me blessed" (Lk 1:48). Blessed are those who honor the Blessed Virgin Mary, mother of all blessings.

6

"Those Who Fear Him"

In her Magnificat, Mary speaks for all Yahweh's poor ones. She praises God and thanks him in their name, because he who is Mighty has responded to her lowliness and also to their neediness. All that God has done for her benefits them. Mary speaks the language of the *anawim* when she says, "His mercy is for those who fear him from generation to generation" (Lk 1:50).

Fear of the Lord finds a place among Yahweh's poor ones, the holy remnant: "O fear the Lord, you his holy ones, for those who fear him have no want" (Ps 34:9). Fear of the Lord includes a deep trust in God and confidence in his generous goodness: "Those who seek the Lord lack no good thing.... Happy are those who take refuge in him" (Ps 34:10, 8).

This trusting relationship with Yahweh, this fear of the Lord, grows out of Israel's past experience of God. First of all, fear of the Lord is a profound reverence for him expressed in adoration, bowing humbly before him. Standing before the fiery holiness of God aflame in the burning bush, "Moses hid his face, for he was afraid to look at God" (Ex 3:6). In reverence for the divine holiness, he took off his shoes. Jacob, too, experienced God's presence and majesty at Bethel and "was afraid, and said, 'How awesome is this place! This is none other than the house of God, and this is the gate of heaven!'" (Gen 28:17).

God does not want to terrify his people, but to reassure them and draw forth from well-disposed hearts a trusting faith, a strong confidence in his merciful goodness. "Fear not!" the Lord reassures us. His majestic holiness may terrify at first, but this holiness surrounds us with loving kindness and mercy: "Fear not!"

God's warning that sin brings its own punishment inspires another kind of fear of the Lord: fear of this punishment. Jesus, the all-merciful one carrying his cross to Calvary, tells us to fear the punishment that comes on the unrepentant sinner: "Then they will begin to say to the mountains, 'Fall on us'; and to the hills, 'Cover us.'" (Lk 23:30). The holiness of God demands deep reverence.

Servile fear, the slavish fear of divine punishment, gives way to filial fear in those who in faith receive the Holy Spirit of the Son: "For you did not receive a spirit of slavery to fall back into fear, but you have received a spirit of adoption. When we cry, 'Abba! Father!' it is that very Spirit bearing witness with our spirit that we are children of God" (Rm 8:15–16). This filial fear of the Lord lovingly reverences God our Father, and trusts him like a child asleep in her father's arms. Filial fear replaces servile fear. "There is no fear in love, but perfect love casts out fear; for fear has to do with punishment, and whoever fears has not reached perfection in love" (1 Jn 4:18). The true lover of God has no fear of divine punishment.

Fear of the Lord is simply the biblical term for a right relationship with God, being right with God. One is fully right with God only when one loves him wholeheartedly and keeps his commandments. This brings happiness: "Happy are those who fear the Lord, who greatly delight in his commandments" (Ps 112:1).

The Book of Deuteronomy emphasizes love as the primary element of fear of the Lord, which is love of God expressed in serving him and obeying his commandments.

Moses says, "Now this is the commandment—the statutes and the ordinances—that the Lord your God charged me to teach you to observe...so that you...may fear the Lord your God all the days of your life and keep all his decrees and his commandments.... You shall love the Lord your God with all your heart" (Dt 6:1–2, 5).

To sum up, fear of the Lord is reverent love of God expressed in faithful service and in obedience to his word. This fear opens us to receive his mercy: "The steadfast love of the Lord is from everlasting to everlasting on those who fear him" (Ps 103:17).

The Holy Spirit bestows the gift of fear, bringing us into this loving relationship with God (cf. Is 11:2). It is both "the beginning of wisdom" and "the crown of wisdom" (Sir 1:14, 18), which consists in this right relationship with God.

Fear of the Lord brings joy and jubilation: "The fear of the Lord is glory and exultation, and gladness and a crown of rejoicing" (Sir 1:11). Experiencing the Lord's mercy in conceiving her Son Jesus, Mary joyously celebrates the mercy God shows to all who fear him.

7

"Mindful of His Mercy"

"His mercy is from age to age to those who fear him" (Lk 1:50 NAB). These words of Mary in her Magnificat clearly echo Psalm 103: "The steadfast love of the Lord is from everlasting to everlasting on those who fear him" (Ps 103:17). Fear of the Lord opens us to God's mercy and compassion.

The first words of the psalm express the same sentiments Mary voiced in opening her Magnificat. The psalm begins, "Bless the Lord, O my soul, and all that is within me, bless his holy name" (v. 1). Mary begins by saying, "My soul magnifies the Lord, and my spirit rejoices in God my Savior" (Lk 1:46). In each case, the singer's whole being praises God, for the word "soul" in Hebrew means the whole living person with all one's vital energy.

Mary's words, "my spirit rejoices" would be better translated, "my spirit exults" or "thrills for joy" or "is enraptured with joy" (Lk 1:46 ZERWICK).

Like the Magnificat, Psalm 103 celebrates God's mercy and compassion. The words "mercy" and "compassion" alternate and interplay throughout the psalm. "Bless the Lord, O my soul...who redeems your life from the pit, who crowns you with steadfast love and mercy *(ḥesed)*.... As a father has *compassion* for his children, so the Lord has *compassion* for those who fear him.... But the *steadfast love* of the Lord is from everlasting to everlasting on those who fear him" (vv. 4, 13, 17).

The Hebrew words for mercy and compassion are often used together, just as mercy and compassion go together in life. While *ḥesed* (mercy) connotes loyalty and fidelity, *raḥamim* highlights the warmth of tenderness and compassion. But the two words are so closely associated that those who translated the Bible into Greek before the coming of Christ rendered *ḥesed*, loyalty, as *eleos*, mercy, because family loyalty shows compassion. The Greek *eleos* in turn became *misericordia* in Latin and "mercy" in English. The Greek text of Mary's Magnificat uses *eleos:* "His mercy is from age to age to those who fear him."

The word *ḥesed* (mercy) originally referred to a basic family quality, for family bonds require family loyalty and mutual support. *Ḥesed* faithfully responds to the neediness of family members. The members all need one another, and *ḥesed* or mercy helps them loyally respond to these needs.

The Hebrew word for compassion *(raḥamim),* used also to signify the womb, expresses a person's instinctive tenderness for those closely bonded to them, such as a mother's tenderness for her infant or a father's for his family. Yahweh, too, uses this word to express his compassion and tender mercy for the people he has made a covenant with. When he makes his covenant with Israel, he accepts them as his family, and uses the Hebrew family vocabulary to express his relationship with them, especially *ḥesed* and *raḥamim*. Thus *ḥesed*, family loyalty, came to mean covenant loyalty or covenant love. It signifies the tender merciful relationship uniting God with his people, and his people among themselves and with God. God showed *ḥesed* toward his people and expected them to show it toward him and one another. Their covenant responsibility demanded this.

Ḥesed always implies loyalty and fidelity. Mercy goes beyond a feeling of compassion (which is unpredictable, since human moods easily change). *Ḥesed* is a consciously willed goodness. This free act of the will springs from an inner sense of duty, of loyalty to others and of fidelity to oneself. For we owe it to self, to our personal integrity, to be faithful to the bonds of family, covenant, friendship, or of other agreements.

God's mercy never acts capriciously. We sing over and over again in the psalms, "Give thanks to the Lord, for his mercy *(ḥesed)* endures forever" (cf., for example, Ps 106:1; 107:1; 136:1–26).

The Covenant of Mercy

Mercy so characterizes God's covenant with his people that "mercy" and "covenant" become almost synonymous. Moses speaks of Yahweh as "the faithful God who keeps covenant and mercy with those who love him and keep his commandments" (Dt 7:9 KJV). The expression "keeps covenant and mercy" is hendiadys, a figure of speech in which two nouns joined by "and" are used instead of a noun and an adjective. "Who keeps covenant and mercy" means "who keeps his merciful covenant."

The covenant relationship began with God's mercy, which impelled him to make the covenant with his people. He chose them without any merit of their own, because of their lowliness and misery. He said to Moses from the burning bush, "I have observed the misery of my people who are in Egypt" (Ex 3:7). Samuel's mother used the word "misery" or "lowliness" *(tapeinosis)* to describe her affliction, as did Mary to describe her lowly state.

God's mercy always responds to human *tapeinosis*—lowliness or neediness. Hence the grateful cry of Mary in her song, "He has looked with favor on the lowliness of his servant" (1:48). Mary echoes Psalm 103, which says, "For he knows how we were made; he remembers that we are dust" (v. 14).

Moved by mercy and compassion, God made his covenant with Israel, binding himself to show mercy to his people forever. God also put mercy at the center of the covenant contract. God bound himself to respond to every need, for mercy faithfully responds to the covenant members who cry out for help. "Give thanks to the Lord, for his mercy *(ḥesed)* endures forever!"

In her Magnificat, Mary celebrates God's fidelity to his merciful covenant, and declares he fulfilled all his covenant promises in the Son she has conceived. God's mercy to Mary is mercy to all his people, for his gift to her is his gift to all. His mercy broadens out to include the whole human race. "For the Mighty One has done great things for me, and holy is his name. His mercy is for those who fear him from generation to generation.... He has helped his servant Israel, in remembrance of his mercy, according to the promise he made to our ancestors, to Abraham and to his descendants forever" (Lk 1:49–50, 54–55).

"In remembrance of his mercy." "To remember," a technical term in the Hebrew Scriptures, is no mere function of the memory. It means to keep one's promises, to be faithful to the covenant. In remembering his mercy, God does not merely call the covenant to mind, but acts on it and keeps it faithfully. Psalm 98 celebrates God's everlasting fidelity to the covenant: "He has remembered his steadfast love *(ḥesed)* and faithfulness to the house of Israel" (v. 3).

The Blessed Virgin Mary herself has trusted in God who remembers: "Blessed is she who believed that there would be a fulfillment of what was spoken to her by the Lord" (1:45). Even the names of Elizabeth and Zechariah celebrate this fidelity of God to his covenant. Elizabeth means "God is my oath," that is, he keeps his promises. Zechariah means "Yahweh has remembered," that is, he has been faithful to his covenant.

God made his covenant of mercy with Israel that they might serve him by bringing his mercy to the whole world. As "the handmaid of the Lord," Mary fulfills this mission and brings mercy to all in giving her Son to the world, and she continues to dispense this mercy as Mother of Mercy. Of course, Jesus is the Servant of divine mercy par excellence. He came not to be served, but to serve, and to give his life as a ransom for the many (cf. Mk 10:45). The salvation that has come into the world in Jesus, Son of Mary, is the ultimate manifestation of God's mercy, the mercy to which he bound himself in making the covenant.

Just as God bound himself to show perpetual mercy, so we too, in entering the covenant with Jesus, bind ourselves to show mercy in all our human relationships. God, who required *ḥesed* of the Israelites in all their dealings with one another, requires it of us: "Blessed are the merciful, for they will receive mercy" (Mt 5:7).

Since only the merciful receive mercy, and God shows mercy to those who fear him, fear of the Lord—right relationship with God—requires that we show mercy. Our covenant relationship with God in Christ obliges us to this. Every intercessor (and every Christian is called to intercede for others) has a mission of mercy to the world, ever begging, "Lord, have mercy!"

8

"Holy Is His Name"

In her Magnificat, the Blessed Virgin Mary uses the vocabulary of the *anawim* and enriches its meaning. She refers to God as mighty, holy and merciful, qualities that the *anawim* loved to attribute to Yahweh. Mary sings, *"The Mighty One"* has done great things for me, and *holy* is his name. His *mercy* is for those who fear him from generation to generation" (Lk 1:49–50). The previous chapter treated God's mercy; this one will treat his power and holiness.

The Mighty One

Announcing God's purpose to form a holy remnant, the *anawim,* Zephaniah calls God the Mighty One, the Savior: "I will leave as a remnant in your midst a people humble and lowly, who shall take refuge in the name of the Lord.... Fear not, O Zion, be not discouraged! The Lord, your God, is in your midst, a mighty Savior" (Zeph 3:12, 16–17 NAB). In her song, Mary attributes both titles to God: "My spirit rejoices in God my Savior...for the *Mighty One* has done great things for me, and holy is his name" (Lk 1:47, 49). He manifests his holiness by his mighty works.

Our Lady enriches the meaning of the three titles she gives to God—mighty, holy, merciful—by showing in her song that God is mightier, holier and more merciful than she had ever imagined. The great things that the Mighty One did for her far exceeded all her hopes.

The Mighty One had looked upon Hannah in her lowliness and barrenness, and she had conceived her son Samuel. But when God looked upon Mary in her lowliness, she conceived her Son virginally, by the power of the Holy Spirit. The mighty God did what is humanly impossible. "For nothing will be impossible with God" (Lk 1:37).

Gabriel had announced this mighty power to Mary: "The Holy Spirit will come upon you, and the power of the Most High will overshadow you" (Lk 1:35). Gabriel speaks in typical Hebrew parallelism, saying the same thing in two ways. The Holy Spirit is that power of the Most High.

Mary, the lowly one, responds by entrusting herself to God: "May it be done to me according to your word" (Lk 1:38 NAB). She then sings in her Magnificat, "The Mighty One has done great things for me, and holy is his name" (1:49). He has done the impossible!

The Virgin Mary contrasts her lowliness with God's might, taking refuge in the Lord (cf. Zeph 3:12) as one of Yahweh's poor and lowly ones. The Mighty One deserves the full trust of the lowly. His merciful power justifies their unshaken hope in him.

Mary's humility sharply contrasts with the proud and arrogant. The Mighty One puts them down from their thrones (cf. 1:51–52), while he exalts the lowly Virgin Mary, so that all generations acclaim her blessed (cf. 1:48). He who is mighty has done this, "and holy is his name" (1:49).

The Holy One

"Holy is his name!" In the great things he has done for her, God's holiness shines forth as never before. Israel's Scriptures emphasize that God shows his holiness by his mighty works of redemption. For example, he gathered his people from among the nations where they were scattered: "I will sanctify my great name, which has been profaned among the nations, and which you have profaned among them;

and the nations shall know that I am the Lord, says the Lord God, when through you I display my holiness before their eyes" (Ez 36:23).

Psalm 111 sounds the same theme: "You won renown for your wondrous deeds.... You sent deliverance to your people, ratified your covenant forever; holy and awesome is your name" (Ps 111:4, 9 NAB).

The child whom Mary conceived by the power of the Most High would so supremely manifest God's holiness that he would be called "the Holy One." Gabriel said to Mary, "The Holy Spirit shall come upon you, and the power of the Most High shall overshadow you. And therefore *the Holy One* who shall be born of thee shall be called Son of God" (1:35 SPENCE). The Latin Vulgate translates it in the same way: *"Ideoque quod nascetur ex te sanctum vocabitur Filius Dei."* In this way of translating, *Holy One* is in apposition with *Son of God:* "Therefore the child to be born will be holy; he will be called Son of God" (1:35).

His holiness is identical with his person as Son of God. His divine conception in Mary's womb reveals God's holiness in an unsurpassed way. Jesus' works will reveal this power and holiness, especially his rising from the dead, with all its redemptive effects. Mary's words, "Holy is his name!" already celebrates all this.

The first Christians recognized Jesus as the Holy One by his mighty deeds. In Peter's Pentecost sermon, he speaks of him as "Jesus of Nazareth, a man attested to you by God with deeds of power, wonders, and signs that God did through him among you, as you yourselves know" (Acts 2:22). Peter calls him "the Holy and Righteous One" (Acts 3:14).

Jesus is called "the Holy One" *(ton hagion)* because, as God's anointed One, he embodies God's mighty power at work, showing the holiness of his name. When the first Christians heard Peter and John's report of their first arrest, they praised God, saying, "...You stretch out your hand to heal, and signs and wonders are performed through the name of your holy servant Jesus" (Acts 4:30).

When Mary says, "The Mighty One has done great things for me" (1:49), she celebrates not only her conception of the Holy One, but also the completion of what God has begun in forming her child in her womb. She speaks about what God will do through this child. She sings of the whole work of redemption. Through the work of her Son, God scatters the proud by the might of his arm; he brings down the powerful from their thrones; he lifts up the lowly.

Mary's words echo Zephaniah who had spoken of God's power scattering the proud: "I will remove from your midst your proudly exultant ones, and you shall no longer be haughty in my holy mountain. For I will leave in the midst of you a people humble and lowly. They shall seek refuge in the name of the Lord—the remnant of Israel" (Zeph 3:11–13).

"The proud" oppose "the humble and lowly" Zephaniah spoke of. Arrogant and overbearing because they do not look up to God, they look down on others.

The psalms also speak often of how the proud oppress the poor, but warn that the proud who rebel against the Lord and his anointed will not prevail. Mary praises the Mighty One, who has done great things for her, for establishing justice.

"He has brought down the powerful from their thrones, and lifted up the lowly; he has filled the hungry with good things, and sent the rich away empty. He has *helped* his servant Israel, in remembrance of his mercy" (1:52–54). The Greek word "helped" literally means "to take in hand, assume the care of" (ZERWICK). This refers to the imagery Yahweh used in speaking to his Servant, "I have taken you by the hand and kept you" (Is 42:6), and to his people Israel, "But you, Israel, my servant...do not fear, for I am with you.... I will uphold you with my victorious right hand" (Is 41:8–10).

In saying, "He has helped his servant Israel" (he has taken him by the hand), the Virgin Mary is referring to these words of Isaiah. In them, Yahweh assures Israel of his faithfulness to the merciful covenant he made with Abraham and with Israel. Mary repeats the metaphor of God's powerful arm which she had already used, saying, "He has shown strength with his arm" (1:51). The powerful arm of God scatters the proud and puts down the mighty, but lovingly takes the lowly by the hand and lifts them up.

Mary then concludes her Magnificat by celebrating God's covenant fidelity: "He has helped his servant Israel, in remembrance of his mercy, according to the promise he made to our ancestors, to Abraham and to his descendants forever" (Lk 1:54–55).

The mercy which the Mighty One has shown to Mary exemplifies the mercy he shows to all of us. What his mercy has done for her shows what he wants to do for his people until the end of time. What he does in us completes what he began for us in Mary's womb.

She declares "All generations will call me blessed" (1:48), because what God has begun in Mary, who represents the *anawim,* he fulfills in "those who fear him from generation to generation" (1:50).

Mary interprets the conception of her Son in light of his redeeming death and resurrection. She says, in effect, "In celebrating the Lord's resurrection, God's supreme work of power, all generations will celebrate with me my conceiving Jesus, the beginning of that work of salvation. They will celebrate the salvation brought to the *anawim* till the end of time."

All that God will ever do for the whole human race "in remembrance of his mercy" (1:54) reached its summit in the great things the Almighty did for Mary in making her the mother of Jesus by the Holy Spirit's power. We praise him in the Magnificat because he is bringing to completion what he began in the Blessed Virgin Mary. Each day at evening prayer in the Liturgy of the Hours, as we sing the Magnificat with Mary, we celebrate all this with her, including what God is doing today in you and in me. He accomplishes these wonders of his mercy in the *anawim*, "those who fear him" (1:50). We praise and thank God together with Mary: "My soul magnifies the Lord, and my spirit rejoices in God my Savior, for he has looked with favor on the lowliness of his servant."

PART THREE

THE EIGHT BEATITUDES

9

The Joy of the Kingdom

"Beatitude" means "perfect happiness." True happiness is a gift from God, a blessing from his goodness. That is why I prefer to translate the beatitudes as "blessed" rather than as "happy."

In each beatitude, Jesus states a certain requirement for receiving this blessing from God, then describes that perfect happiness. For example, genuine happiness consists in seeing God, and seeing God requires purity of heart. Again, happiness consists in possessing the kingdom of God, and possessing the kingdom requires poverty of spirit.

In the beatitudes, Jesus presents various qualities of life in that kingdom, different aspects of its perfect happiness. In the kingdom, all who have mourned will find their tears wiped away; those who hunger and thirst for justice will find it; the merciful will receive God's mercy. The kingdom will bring the joy of being with God and seeing him in his glory. There, all God's children will dwell together, at home in their Father's house, enjoying one another in peace. Although the happiness of the beatitudes will be perfect only in heaven, it begins even on earth for those who live its demands.

These requirements for entering the Father's joy in the kingdom call us to a new way of life. They provide the moral foundation for fullness of life in the Holy Spirit. This doesn't mean that the beatitudes require only observing the moral law or practicing the virtues such as temperance and justice. The beatitudes do not give specific details about things to do or virtues to practice. No, they go deeper than that.

The requirements of the beatitudes are basic life attitudes. They form our fundamental outlook so that our way of living springs from them. They orient the human heart toward true happiness. We can begin to taste this happiness now, although in this life it will never be perfect. The beatitudes "promise fullness of life in God's kingdom. They are primarily eschatological, though there may be some anticipation of the reward in the present" (HARRINGTON, p. 83).

In presenting the beatitudes, Jesus puts before us this true goal of life. In telling us how to find happiness, Jesus shows us how our whole being strives toward this authentic happiness. God bestows this peace of heart on those who are rightly disposed to receive it by doing what Jesus asks.

Beatitude consists in possessing God in intimate union. The beatitudes show us how to be open to receive God's blessings. Humble openness to God's action in our lives builds a strong foundation for Christian living, like a house built on rock that can withstand even a hurricane (cf. Mt 7:24–27). This receptivity, this trusting hope in God, expects everything from him.

Though they utterly depend on God, those who live the eight beatitudes are not weaklings. They are strong and courageous, the strongest of the strong. Yet this presupposes that we know our profound neediness and utter poverty before God. When we experience our littleness as children before God, the humility of the poor in spirit will grow in us. Jesus will bless us as he did the children who came to him: "He took them up in his arms, laid his hands on them, and blessed them" (Mk 10:16).

Joyfully accepting Jesus, our saving God present among

us, opens us to receive the beatitude only God can give. We are blessed, happy, joyful, because Jesus the messiah brings us the beatitude of the kingdom. The poor and needy, the sorrowful and the persecuted, find happiness and blessing because God cares about them, providing for their needs.

In its literary form, a beatitude expresses joy over another's good fortune. Beatitudes "do not confer a blessing but recognize an existing state of happiness or blessing; they are an approving proclamation, often signifying that eschatological joy has come" (BROWN, p. 333, note 42). Thus Elizabeth cries out to Mary, "Blessed are you who believed that what was spoken to you by the Lord would be fulfilled" (Lk 1:45 NAB). Luke's version makes it clear that the beatitudes are cries of congratulation. In Luke's Gospel, Jesus congratulates the poor and needy. He addresses them directly, saying:

> Blessed are you who are poor...
> Blessed are you who are hungry now...
> Blessed are you who weep now...
> Blessed are you when people hate you... (Lk 6:20–22).

You poor, you hungry, you sorrowing, you who are persecuted can rejoice because God cares about you. Jesus, the messiah sent by God, responds to your poverty and hunger, your weeping and oppression.

The Sermon on the Mount thus begins with a cry of joy that the messiah has brought the kingdom of God near. In eight ways, the beatitudes cry out our joyful, grateful acceptance of our saving God. The beatitudes call for joyful hope. In our poverty and neediness, we open ourselves wide to God's saving presence in Christ, trusting he will take care of us. "Open your mouth wide and I will fill it" (Ps 81:10).

Ultimately, we need the salvation Christ gives not only because we are creatures, but because we are sinners. Our most dire neediness stems from sin, which cuts us off from God, who gives us life and well-being. "Just as the branch cannot bear fruit by itself unless it abides in the vine, neither can you unless you abide in me" (Jn 15:4).

In our neediness as little ones, we totally depend on God our Father in trust and hope. We hunger and thirst for the righteousness that God alone can give. We look to him for consolation when life disappoints us, knowing our present life cannot bring perfect happiness. We reach out to God in our sinful failures and hope for mercy.

The beatitudes essentially call for openness to God in faith, hope and trust, so that *he* can be our beatitude. The morality of the beatitudes hinges on developing the theological virtues of faith, hope and charity. These three form our fundamental moral stance.

Secondarily, the beatitudes also involve practicing the moral virtues, beginning with humility and meekness. These characterize our hope in God. Because we trust so completely in God we can be meek and gentle toward all, free from vindictive anger. Because we trust in God our mourning is tempered by patience and the joy of hope. Trust in God leads to the temperance that uses food, drink and sex as God intends, without making them the center of our lives. Trusting in God and his care for us makes it much easier to deal justly with others, for we do not rely on lying, cheating and stealing. All these virtues work together to bring about the purity of heart necessary for seeing God.

Community Aspects of the Beatitudes

The beatitudes are not individualistic, but characterize God's people as community. All eight deal with relationships with God and with neighbor. The poor in spirit, like little children humbly trusting in God their Father, reach out to their brothers and sisters, God's children. The poor in spirit are not proud and arrogant, imposing themselves on others. They are peacemakers, living in harmony with all God's children. They quickly forgive anyone who seeks their forgiveness. They are meek and gentle toward all, free of hatred and resentment, merciful and compassionate, open to all in kindness and goodness. They "rejoice with those who rejoice, weep with those who weep" (Rm 12:15). They bring the consolation and peace of God to one another. The beatitude of mourning is a shared weeping, just as Jesus shared all our sorrows. It supports others in their troubles. Jesus did what Isaiah spoke of, "He took our infirmities and bore our diseases" (Mt 8:17). God calls all of us to act as Jesus did. "Bear one another's burdens, and in this way you will fulfill the law of Christ" (Gal 6:2).

The beatitudes are fruits of the Holy Spirit, who works in us because we belong to Christ. "The fruit of the Spirit is love, joy, peace, patience, kindness, generosity, faithfulness, gentleness, and self-control" (Gal 5:22–23). Certainly all of these are community virtues.

Wholeheartedness toward God

The beatitudes do not call for the "do it yourself" perfection the Greek philosophers described. Authentic biblical holiness comes from wholeheartedness toward God, the wholehearted yielding of self to God alone in openness to his saving grace.

In the Hebrew Scriptures, God asked his people first of all not for refined moral perfection, but faith and trust in him, so that he could gradually lead them to an ever more refined morality. He asked Abraham: "Walk in my presence and be wholehearted" (Gen 17:1 AUTHOR). The word *tamim,* which I have translated as "wholehearted" rather than as "blameless," derives from a root word meaning "whole, complete, sound." A human person is whole, complete, only when he or she has a right relationship with God. To be wholehearted toward God is to be single heartedly dedicated to him, not having a divided heart given to other gods besides him, for Yahweh alone is God.

God's basic requirement of Abraham was: be faithful to me, the one and only God. "Walk in my presence and be whole-hearted."

Once we have given ourselves to God in wholehearted devotion, he can guide us step by step to holiness. The eight beatitudes present different elements of this whole-hearted relationship with God. We surrender to him so that he can fill us with the blessings of the kingdom.

The beatitudes, then, briefly describe these blessings, and focus our attention on the basic attitudes necessary to receive the kingdom. The rest of Matthew's Gospel will present the kingdom in greater detail, and show more precisely the conditions for entering it.

10

God's Reign on Earth

Knowing their neediness before God, and because of the injustices they suffered, Yahweh's poor had long been looking forward to the reign of God. They expected that God's reign would effectively establish justice on earth. Why then does Matthew's Gospel say of them, "Blessed are the poor in spirit, for theirs is *the kingdom of heaven*" (5:3)?

The word "heaven" as used here is a reverent circumlocution for Yahweh's holy name. This was a common Jewish manner of speech at that time. Out of respect for the all-holy God, people did not dare to pronounce his name. They would substitute another word, such as "heaven," for the holy name Yahweh. Whenever a person reading the Scriptures would come across the name Yahweh, he or she would substitute the word *Adonai* (my Lord). When the Scriptures were translated into Greek, the word *Kyrios* (Lord) was used in place of Yahweh, out of profound reverence for the divine name. Even today many English Bibles have lord, in four capital letters, instead of the name Yahweh. Whenever LORD appears in our English text, the original Hebrew had yhwh (Yahweh).

Out of reverence, the author of the First Book of Maccabees avoided the word "God," and used "heaven" instead. "They cried aloud to heaven" (3:50); "In the sight of heaven, there is no difference between saving by many or by few" (3:18). Likewise, in the parable Jesus told, the prodigal son says to his father, "Father, I have sinned against heaven and before you" (Lk 15:21).

On reading Matthew's expression, "the kingdom of heaven is theirs," the early Christians of Jewish background would have understood immediately that Matthew meant God's kingdom come down on earth. The spiritually-minded Jewish people were looking forward to just that: God's rule on earth. The reign of God they were expecting was God's sovereignty in establishing justice and peace on earth as in heaven. Jesus approved this idea, for he taught us to pray, "Your kingdom come. Your will be done, on earth as it is in heaven" (Mt 6:10).

Unfortunately, the expression "the kingdom of heaven" has been misleading for a great many Christian readers of later times, who did not know that "heaven" was a reverent substitute for God's holy name. For them, "heaven" means only the next life. But in Matthew's Gospel, "the kingdom of heaven" means Yahweh's rule over people, and so his reign even on earth.

This is a very important point for accurately interpreting the beatitudes. Jesus did not preach an irreconcilable opposition between earth and heaven. To a superficial reader, it may seem the beatitudes stress an antithesis: poverty now, the kingdom later; mourning now, comfort in the next life; hunger and thirst now, fullness in heaven. The beatitudes, however, do not teach that salvation and happiness come only in the next life. They do not say, "Life on earth is hopeless, your only hope is in the afterlife; suffer patiently now, and heaven will be yours in due time."

Christianity has often been accused of such a doctrine, of having no concern for the poor and miserable, no interest in the human values of this world. Karl Marx called its promise of a life hereafter an "opiate of the people," meant to drug them so that they will let the wealthy oppress them. Atheistic humanism, in its professed concern for the poor here and now, has won a large following because too many Christians have not understood or lived the beatitudes.

According to the Jewish Scriptures, the kingdom of God originates in heaven, but comes down to earth: "I saw one like a son of man coming with the clouds of heaven. And he came to the Ancient One and was presented before him. To him was given dominion and glory and kingship, that all peoples, nations, and languages should serve him" (Dan 7:13). The peoples of the earth are subject to him who receives kingship from the heavenly Ancient One.

People have often misinterpreted what Jesus said to Pilate about the kingdom, thinking it means that the kingdom does not come on earth. In an older translation Jesus says, "My kingdom is not *of* this world." A more accurate translation is, "My kingdom is not *from* this world" (Jn 18:36). Its origin and authority come from above, but its rule is on earth, among the people who accept Christ the king.

According to the beatitudes, salvation and grace, the messianic gift of happiness, are already at work on earth. We find happiness even now to the extent that God reigns in the world by reigning in human hearts. The messiah cares about the poor of this world and about improving their condition: "Go and tell John what you hear and see: the blind receive their sight, the lame walk, the lepers are cleansed, the deaf hear, the dead are raised, and the poor have good news brought to them" (Mt 11:4–5). The messiah has come to bless Yahweh's poor ones.

Though the happiness proclaimed in the beatitudes will be complete and perfect only in the next life, it truly begins in this life for those who live the beatitudes. In discussing each of them, I shall try to show how we can

live, by the grace of Christ, the life of that beatitude even
now on earth.

What Is the Kingdom of God?

To understand how we can begin to live and enjoy the
blessings of the beatitudes even on earth, we need to
understand what the Scriptures mean by the "reign of
God" as Jesus preached it: "Now after John was arrested,
Jesus came to Galilee, proclaiming the good news of God,
and saying, 'The time is fulfilled, and the kingdom of God
has come near; repent, and believe in the good news'"
(Mk 1:14–15).

Jesus does not say, "The kingdom is here," but "The
kingdom is near." The time is fulfilled. Under God's power
and guidance, history moves toward its God-given goal.
The old order must give place to the new order, the reign of
God. The reign is close at hand, but not yet here.

Because it is still largely in the future, Jesus urges us to
pray, "Your kingdom come, your will be done on earth as it
is in heaven." We are to pray that God's will for justice and
holiness be realized as perfectly on earth as it is in heaven.

But isn't the kingdom already present in an initial way in
the person and power of Christ? "If it is by the Spirit of God
that I cast out demons, then the kingdom of God has come
to you" (Mt 12:28; cf. Lk 17:21). If the power of the kingdom already works in the world in the Person and Spirit of
Jesus, then we should be open to this power in poverty of
spirit, and expect many of its effects in our lives here and
now. The kingdom will not come to its final completion in
the next life unless it has already begun in our hearts and
lives now on earth. To the extent that we respond to the
presence and power of Jesus by living the beatitudes, the
kingdom is here, and we can begin to enjoy its blessings.

"The kingdom" is a symbol for all the blessings Jesus

brings. The eight beatitudes sum up these blessings, which will be completed in us in heaven only because they have begun in us on earth.

In preaching that the kingdom of God is near at hand, Jesus spells out what it demands: "Repent, and believe in the good news!" (Mk 1:15). The kingdom comes where people do God's will. The first condition for entering the kingdom is "Repent!" Repent of past injustices, turn to God's will and live accordingly.

The second condition is "Believe in the good news!" The kingdom is God's work as he establishes his will for righteousness in the world. To believe is to yield oneself to this power and grace. The eight beatitudes describe in more detail what it means to repent and to believe. For example, those who repent of their sins are the blessed mournful; the poor in spirit entrust themselves in faith to the Lord, their only hope. The good news is the presence of the messiah, who fulfills all the hopes of the *anawim,* who hunger and thirst for righteousness.

In Luke's Gospel, Jesus proclaims the kingdom in a different way than he does in Mark. In Mark, he simply says, "Repent, and believe in the good news" (1:15). Luke's version elaborates on this. Jesus announces his agenda, saying, "The Spirit of the Lord is upon me, because he has anointed me to bring *good news to the poor.* He has sent me to proclaim release to the captives and recovery of sight to the blind, to let the oppressed go free, to proclaim the year of the Lord's favor" (Lk 4:18–19). This passage describes what the kingdom of God come to earth means. God's reign will bring justice to the oppressed, the Lord's poor and needy ones, and release those who mourn their sinfulness.

St. Paul gives us an especially clear description of the kingdom: "The kingdom of God is not food and drink but righteousness and peace and joy in the Holy Spirit" (Rm 14:17).

That all this begins even on earth is clear from the Lord's statement, "The kingdom of God is among you" (Lk 17:21). This means that the kingdom is at work in the saving power and healing deeds of Jesus. But the present working of the kingdom is only a beginning. After stating "the kingdom of God is among you," Jesus goes on to talk about the completion of the reign of God when the Son of Man comes in glory (cf. Lk 17:22–37).

Where is the reign of God already at work on earth? Wherever God is at work in human relationships, bringing people together so that we may love one another. When the scribe so beautifully said to Jesus, "'To love him with all the heart, and with all the understanding, and with all the strength,' and 'to love one's neighbor as oneself'—this is much more important than all whole burnt offerings and sacrifices," Jesus praised him, "You are not far from the kingdom of God" (Mk 12:33–34).

If to *know* the great commandment of love of God and neighbor is to be close to the kingdom, then surely to *keep* that commandment is to be in the reign of God. In the great judgment scene in Matthew's Gospel, those who enter the final glory of the kingdom are those who have fed the hungry, clothed the naked, sheltered the homeless: "I was hungry, and you gave me food.... As often as you did it to the least of these my brothers and sisters, you did it to me" (Mt 25:35 f.).

Do not the eight beatitudes simply express different aspects of our right relationship with God and neighbor in love? In the measure that even on earth we already live the beatitude described, in due time we will enjoy the complete and perfect beatitude of heaven.

The preceding chapter stated that the beatitudes call for a new way of life; all our living should spring from their dynamism. To the degree that we live this way of life, we begin to enjoy even on earth the blessings the beatitudes bring. Jesus says of the blessed poor in spirit: "Theirs is the kingdom of heaven."

11

The Poor in Spirit

Blessed are the poor in spirit,
for theirs is the kingdom of heaven (Mt 5:3).

The Beatitudes: Openness to the Messiah

The eight beatitudes can be best understood only in light of the spirituality of the *anawim*, the full flowering of Israel's spirituality. Experiencing their poverty and neediness, their sinfulness and helplessness, the people learned to trust in Yahweh alone and to wait for him in hope. They looked to him to relieve their pain. Their spirituality developed into openness to the promised messiah, whom they hoped for.

The messiah comes in response to their prayers and longings. They are blessed because of their humility and meekness, their mourning over sin, their hunger and thirst for righteousness, their purity of heart, purified in suffering. These attitudes open them to receive the messiah and the blessings he brings. They are blessed because they receive him, the giver of all spiritual blessings.

The spirituality of the *anawim* reached its perfection during the Babylonian exile and the painful difficulties after the return from the exile. During that time of restoration, a prophet called Trito-Isaiah preached. (The third part of the

Book of Isaiah, chapters 56–66, derive from him and his community.) Obviously one of the *anawim,* his words give us a deep insight into the meaning of the beatitudes, especially "Blessed are the poor in spirit" and "Blessed are those who mourn." He presents the messiah as one who will preach good news to the poor and will comfort all who mourn:

> The spirit of the Lord is upon me,
>> because the Lord has anointed me;
> he has sent me to bring good news to the
>> oppressed *(anawim),*
>> to bind up the brokenhearted,
> to proclaim liberty to the captives,
>> and release to the prisoners;
> to proclaim the year of the Lord's favor,
>> and the day of vengeance of our God;
>> to comfort all who mourn,
> to provide for those who mourn in Zion—
>> to give them a garland instead of ashes,
> the oil of gladness instead of mourning,
>> the mantle of praise instead of a faint spirit.
> They will be called oaks of righteousness,
>> the planting of the Lord, to display his glory....
> All who see them shall acknowledge
>> that they are a people whom the Lord has
>> blessed (Is 61:1–3, 9).

Jesus read this passage aloud in the synagogue at Nazareth, and then said, "Today this scripture has been fulfilled in your hearing" (Lk 4:21). Jesus brings all the blessings of the beatitudes. All who have the attitudes that the beatitudes describe are blessed because the messiah is here to respond to their neediness.

The words of Trito-Isaiah quoted above comforted the people after the exile. They mourned not just over their sins, but over all the evils that followed in sin's wake. They grieved over the hardships and disillusionments of those terribly difficult days of restoration, days of rebuilding not only the destroyed city of Jerusalem, but renewing the community of God's people.

As they tried to restore a shattered nation, they suffered physical poverty too. But for the prophet, the word "poor" also has a spiritual meaning, a resonance that echoes again in two other passages. From these texts, we learn that we can respond to the majestic holiness of God through poverty of spirit or humility and mourning over sin:

> For thus says the high and lofty one
>> who inhabits eternity, whose name is Holy:
> I dwell in the high and holy place,
>> and also with those who are
>> contrite and humble in spirit,
> to revive the spirit of the humble,
>> and to revive the heart of the contrite (Is 57:15).

The people fall on their knees and beat their breasts before God's holiness and infinite majesty. The all-holy God dwells with those of humble and contrite spirit, to console the heart of the contrite and vivify the spirit of the humble.

When Jesus says, "Blessed are the poor in spirit, blessed are those who mourn" with humble and contrite hearts, he means that he comforts them and revives them *by his saving presence,* by the forgiveness he grants them, and *by dwelling with them.* The poor in spirit, those who sorrow for sin, the hungry and thirsty for righteousness, are blessed because the messiah has come.

Fear of the Lord

Poverty of spirit brings openness to the all-holy God in reverence and humility, with contrition for sin and ready obedience to his word. The scriptural term, "Fear of the Lord" expresses these essential elements. These traits characterize "the little ones," the poor in spirit, as children of

God. They experience the all-holy God as a merciful and compassionate Father. They have a relationship of filial reverence with the Father, the Lord of heaven and earth. This reverence, filled with tender love, is the positive side of poverty of spirit.

That is why St. Thomas Aquinas teaches that the Holy Spirit's gift of fear perfects our poverty of spirit. Thomas means filial fear, a child's loving reverence for his or her parents, not servile fear, a slave's fear of punishment. "For you did not receive a spirit of slavery to fall back into fear, but you have received a spirit of adoption. When we cry, 'Abba! Father!' it is that very Spirit bearing witness with our spirit that we are children of God" (Rm 8:15–16). The Holy Spirit's gift of filial fear inspires in us a fear of our own weakness and proneness to sin that may cause us to offend our beloved Father. In this fear of our own weakness, we learn to trust more completely in God our Father.

The best explanation of the first beatitude, "Blessed are the poor in spirit, for theirs is the kingdom of heaven," is found in Jesus' other words, "Truly I tell you, unless you change and become like children, you will never enter the kingdom of heaven" (Mt 18:3). Jesus had called a little child to himself. Placing the child in their midst, he presented the little one as the symbol of the true disciple, saying, "Unless you change" by conversion of heart "and become like children, you will never enter the kingdom of heaven." The poor in spirit are those who through conversion have become like little children.

This conversion turns one away from pride, self-centeredness, self-sufficiency, and toward the Father in child-like trust. Jesus adds immediately, "Whoever becomes humble like this child is the greatest in the kingdom of heaven" (Mt 18:4).

What essential quality of children makes them symbolize discipleship? It isn't innocence, for everyone knows how difficult children can be at times. Rather, it is that they know their neediness and helplessness. Children run to their parents when they need something. Similarly, one must run to God, admitting one's helplessness and need for salvation. One becomes like a little child through conversion, humbling self in repentance, and trusting in God, who alone can save.

Straying Sheep

The disciples of Christ, the "little ones," still tend to sin, to stray, even after their initial conversion to Jesus. So he seeks them even as the shepherd seeks the lost sheep.

How are we to treat those disciples who stray into sin? Are we to despise and abandon them, leaving them to their misery, saying that they deserve what they get? Not at all. The Father still cherishes these little ones, so precious to him. "Take care that you do not despise one of these little ones; for, I tell you, in heaven their angels continually see the face of my Father in heaven" (Mt 18:10). The Father so cares for them that he has assigned each of them an angel to bring them safely home into his presence.

We so often use this text to tell little children that they have guardian angels that we might forget that Jesus here speaks of adults also. Our Lord designates every authentic disciple as a "little one." In this particular passage, "little one" means any disciple of any age, who in human weakness can fall into sin. Poverty of spirit, true humility, thus includes a healthy fear of one's weakness, one's capacity for straying into sin.

When Jesus presents the parable of the good shepherd, he carefully encloses it between two references to "little ones," meaning his disciples, who tend to go astray:

> . Take care that you do not despise one of these little
> ones; for I tell you, in heaven their angels continu-
> ally see the face of my Father in heaven. What do

> you think? If a shepherd has a hundred sheep, and
> one of them has gone astray, does he not leave the
> ninety-nine on the mountains and go in search of
> the one that went astray? And if he finds it, truly I
> tell you, he rejoices over it more that over the
> ninety-nine that never went astray. So it is not the
> will of your Father in heaven that one of these little
> ones should be lost (Mt 18:10–14).

The Father cherishes "the little ones," the disciples who stray into sin, and asks us to do the same. Like the good shepherd, the other disciples are to seek them and lovingly receive them back into the fold.

Even if they haven't gone astray, the disciples, the spiritual little ones, recognize that they are as helpless as lost sheep and can go astray. They can't gain salvation on their own. Poverty of spirit, true humility, recognizes and accepts this, trusting in God rather than in self. One will not go astray if one is poor in spirit, humbly recognizes one's weakness, and hopes in the Lord. Poverty of spirit involves both a humble acceptance of one's neediness, and a positive hope in God.

The poor in spirit live a very real poverty. If hope in God does not sustain their helplessness, it is far more disastrous than the physical poverty of having no material goods. This poverty is the lack of power and resources to save oneself and come into the kingdom, which is God's gift. True poverty of spirit includes hope in God. We cannot get to God by our own power, no more than a car can run without gas.

Empty before God, the poor in spirit are open to receive the blessing of the kingdom. "Blessed are the poor in spirit, for theirs is the kingdom of heaven."

Since the essence of spiritual childhood is not innocence or sinlessness, but trust in God, sinners have great hope. If they turn and repent, humbling themselves before God's mercy, they will receive the kingdom. It comes as the gift of

God's compassionate love for the little ones, his weak and lowly repentant children.

Poverty of spirit is sometimes explained as detachment from material goods. But poverty of spirit is far more basic than mere detachment from riches. It means to recognize and accept that of ourselves we are helpless to reach God, and need to trust humbly in him. Poverty of spirit opens a person in faith and hope to the presence and power of God. Both the materially rich and poor need this spiritual poverty. When materially wealthy persons are truly poor in spirit, trusting wholly in God, then they do not center their lives on material goods. Their generous mercy in using their resources in helping the needy shows this detachment.

The Millstone

Recognizing the fragility of the "little ones," the Lord's disciples beware of giving scandal. We appreciate Jesus' stern warning, "If any of you put a stumbling block before one of these little ones who believe in me, it would be better for you if a great millstone were fastened around your neck and you were drowned in the depth of the sea" (Mt 18:6).

We need to recognize the fragility and human weakness of our fellow believers and do nothing to tempt anyone in the least way. By carefully avoiding anything that might lead others to sin, we take seriously the Lord's warning, "Woe to the world because of stumbling blocks! Occasions for stumbling are bound to come, but woe to the one by whom the stumbling block comes!" (Mt 18:7). We are responsible to God for the example we set for other people. By living the beatitudes we can influence others for the good.

12

The Mournful

Blessed are those who mourn,
for they will be comforted (Mt 5:4).

The Blessing of Mourning

Is it a blessing to weep and mourn? Not every kind of mourning brings us blessings or leads to happiness. But mourning can bring blessings if we mourn for the right things, for the right reasons, and with the right attitudes.

What sort of evils should we mourn over? The beatitude of mourning concerns not only sin, but all the sufferings of life. We mourn over physical evils such as cancer, blindness, poverty, death, violence, crime, family troubles and the like. Even Jesus wept with Mary and Martha when his friend Lazarus died (cf. Jn 11:35). Every kind of human suffering moved Jesus to compassion.

Just as we rejoice over all the good things God has given us and thank him sincerely for them, so we can feel sad when we lack these goods. It's natural to feel sad when we face a long hospital stay, or have no one to celebrate Thanksgiving or Christmas with, or have a stack of bills and no money in the bank. Sadness is a human, God-given emotion.

But virtues regulate our expression of emotion, like an officer directing traffic. Anger is to be regulated by meekness, ambition by humility, sexual desires by chastity, fear by courage, and so on. Patience is the special virtue in charge of sadness. When we feel sad, patience can manage sadness so it doesn't go uncontrolled.

The key to managing sadness lies in how one judges the evil one is enduring. There are degrees of evil. The only evil pure and simple is loss of God, separation from him. Other evils are evil only in some limited respect, and so should elicit different degrees of sadness. Only loss of God deserves sadness unlimited. The virtue of patience helps one put in proper perspective the evil that gives rise to sadness.

Since sadness over evil comes into every human life, blessed mourning concerns not only sin, but all the miseries of human life. It is largely a matter of attitude. It depends on how we look at our troubles and respond to them. Mourning over misery can open us to God in hope and trust, and thus bring blessings. Or it can close us to God and to others, and lead us to sin. For example, self-pity can poison our attitude toward life's difficulties. The beatitude of mourning has nothing to do with self-pity, which can leave us like dried up old prunes.

The mourning that brings blessings does not resent God or neighbor. With patience it trusts in God, hopes in sorrow, and believes in God's love and concern.

The beatitude of mourning relates to the first and third beatitudes, for it is another aspect of humility and meekness. The poor in spirit are blessed in mourning, for in their sorrow they humbly hope in God and find comfort in him. The meek and gentle are also blessed in mourning, because they deal with their troubles without resentment, knowing that God works everything for the good of those who love him (cf. Rm 8:28).

The blessed ones who mourn, then, are the poor of the first beatitude, and the meek of the third. Like various facets of one jewel, each beatitude brings out different aspects of "the little ones." All of them express elements of *anawim* spirituality. In the passage from Isaiah which Jesus applied to himself in the synagogue at Nazareth, "the poor" and "the contrite of heart" refer to the same persons; the second line of the parallelism explains the first:

> He has sent me to bring good news to the poor,
>   to bind up the brokenhearted (Is 61:1).

The word "brokenhearted" has given rise to the word "contrite" (from the Latin *contritus,* broken), meaning sorrowful over sin and repentant. In Isaiah's context, brokenheartedness seems to refer primarily to sin, and also to the miseries that flow from it.

The beatitude of mourning deals primarily with poverty as sorrow for sin, as being poor before God. Mourning means knowing that one needs grace and forgiveness, because one has wasted his or her heritage like the prodigal son sitting among pigs, starving. While it expresses neediness, this poverty of contrition also hopes in the Father of mercies for the life and salvation he gives to the repentant. "The poor have the good news preached to them" means that they hear the good news of forgiveness.

In bringing this good news, the messiah comforts those who mourn: "The spirit of the Lord God is upon me, because the Lord has anointed me; he has sent me to bring good news to the oppressed, to bind up the brokenhearted...to comfort all who mourn" (Is 61:1–2).

The *anawim,* Yahweh's poor ones, mourned especially during the Babylonian exile, not merely over their sufferings, but with contrition for the sins that had brought on these sufferings. The Book of Consolation (Isaiah 40–55) was directed especially to them:

Comfort, O comfort my people,
  says your God.
Speak tenderly to Jerusalem,
  and cry to her
that she has served her term,
  that her penalty is paid,
that she has received from the Lord's hand
  double for all her sins (Is 40:1–2).

The prophets persistently proclaimed that in the messianic kingdom joy would replace suffering and tears, and death itself would disappear: "He will swallow up death forever. Then the Lord God will wipe away the tears from all faces, and the disgrace of his people he will take away from all the earth, for the Lord has spoken" (Is 25:7–8). "I am about to create Jerusalem as a joy, and its people as a delight. I will rejoice in Jerusalem, and delight in my people; no more shall the sound of weeping be heard in it, or the cry of distress" (Is 65:18–19).

Matthew's Gospel often presents Jesus as the comforting Servant of Yahweh: "He will not break a bruised reed or quench a smoldering wick" (Mt 12:20; Is 42:3). "He took our infirmities and bore our diseases" (Mt 8:17; Is 53:4).

On the lips of Jesus, the beatitudes announce the fulfillment of all the hopes of Yahweh's contrite poor ones. The beatitudes bring the blessings of God's own joy to the poor and lowly who mourn: "I have said these things to you so that my joy may be in you, and that your joy may be complete" (Jn 15:11).

Mourning over Injustice

Thus far this chapter has highlighted mourning as contrition for sin. But in the passage Jesus quoted at Nazareth, the messiah declares that he will comfort also those who mourn over the injustices they endure. He will set these wrongs right. He will vindicate them against their oppressors. Especially in the psalms, Yahweh's poor ones often cry out for such vindication, such righting of wrongs. They do not take revenge into their own hands, but cry out to God to vindicate them against their oppressors.

Never vengeful toward those who cause their sufferings, the blessed ones who mourn expect justice from God. "They will receive blessing from the Lord, and vindication from the God of their salvation" (Ps 24:5). They hunger and thirst for the justice only God can establish, for "anger does not produce God's righteousness" (Jas 1:20).

Sharing in the Mourning of Others

The poor in spirit, meek and gentle of heart, also mourn over the evils other people suffer. With compassion and mercy, they "weep with those who weep" (Rm 12:15).

If I am proud and hardhearted toward others, I will not care about the misery of the world about me, and least of all its spiritual misery. An unrepentant sinner will hardly shed tears of sorrow over the sins of others.

But if I humbly experience my own neediness before God, and if I am meek, gentle and compassionate toward others, I will deeply mourn over their miseries. I will weep with those who weep. I will reach out to them in love and concern, like Jesus who wept with Martha and Mary when their brother Lazarus died (cf. Jn 11:33–35). Blessed mourning knows love's solidarity with others in their suffering, and comforts those who mourn. From the depths of his own suffering, which included imprisonment, scourging, stoning and shipwreck (cf. 2 Cor 11:23–33), St. Paul comforted others in their sorrows: "Blessed be the God and Father of our Lord Jesus Christ, the Father of mercies and the God of all consolation, who consoles us in all our affliction, so that we may be able to console those who are in any affliction with the consolation with which we ourselves are consoled by God" (2 Cor 1:3–4).

Carrying his cross to Calvary, with blood flowing from his own wounds, Jesus felt concern for the women who wept for him. "Daughters of Jerusalem, do not weep for me, but weep for yourselves and for your children" (Lk 23:28). Jesus did not indulge in self-pity. He suffered willingly so that these women and their children could be relieved of the miseries caused by sin. But they must mourn for their sins, and so receive the blessed comfort of forgiveness. Jesus understood the deepest misery of all, the misery of sin, although he never sinned. I must mourn over my sins in repentance, and let the Lord comfort me by reconciliation with God and others.

Jesus lived out what Isaiah had spoken of, "He took our infirmities and bore our diseases" (Mt 8:17). All of us are to imitate Jesus. "Bear one another's burdens, and in this way you will fulfill the law of Christ" (Gal 6:2).

"They will be comforted." In whatever distress we find ourselves, even distress over our sins, we find peace in humbly accepting the Lord's merciful forgiveness, glorifying his merciful love, and suffering other trials in patient reparation for sin. Contrition for sin brings happiness. We can rest in God's merciful love and enjoy his friendship.

Comforted on Earth

In heaven God will dry all our tears. "God himself will be with them; he will wipe away every tear from their eyes. Death will be no more; mourning and crying and pain will be no more, for the first things have passed away" (Rev 21:3–4).

Can we enjoy only in heaven the comfort given to those who mourn? Does enjoying this beatitude on earth require conquering all evil? When we mourn over the evil effects of sin, how can this beatitude comfort us while these evil effects still afflict us?

This beatitude often comforts us not by removing the evil, but by giving us courage to bear it with patience and even joy: "Whenever you face trials of any kind, consider it nothing but joy, because you know that the testing of your faith produces endurance; and let endurance have its full effect, so that you may be mature and complete, lacking in nothing" (Jas 1:2–4).

Mourning over Sin and Its Effects

Certainly when one mourns over one's sins, consolation comes only when true repentance removes this evil. God's grace of forgiveness wipes out our sin. Peace with God and the joy of reconciliation comfort the sinner. Yet the fullness of comfort that mourning brings also requires removing the evil effects left in the forgiven sinner. For example, a spouse who has committed adultery has damaged the love of their marriage covenant and needs to repair the harm done.

Sin not only offends God, it hurts the sinner. Sin offends God because it spoils the beautiful creature God created us to be. It distorts God's image in us and lessens the glory our goodness and holiness would give him.

Besides distorting God's image in us, sin puts barriers between us and God that hinder our receiving God's life-giving love. The bad habits formed by repeated sin make it difficult to practice virtue even when we have sincerely repented. A person who has formed a habit of lying will find it hard to always tell the truth. Penitential practices and doing good works of love can help to heal these evil effects.

Enjoying the fullness of consolation first requires healing the wounds of our sins. We punish ourselves by sinning, through its evil effects, as when a hangover follows a bout of drunkenness. But we can change this punishment into reparation for sin by suffering it patiently for love of God. When we admit our guilt and accept responsibility for our sin, we can enjoy the comfort that comes from forgiveness and from repairing the harm we have done.

True contrition springs from humbly admitting guilt and accepting responsibility for our sin and its effects. Compunction over the evil effects of our sins can continue even after we have received forgiveness. We no longer mourn over our guilt, because God's forgiveness has blotted it out, but we feel sorrow over sin's consequences. We strive as best we can to repair the damage, making reparation by good works of love and penance. Our mourning will then win the fullness of comfort.

Sometimes we suffer deeply from the evil effects caused by the sins of others, such as loved ones caught in a web of sin. For example, a mother may suffer deep distress because her husband's sins against their children have deeply wounded them. Sinful effects like these can affect many generations and cause untold suffering in many family members. How can the beatitude promised to those who mourn come to those loving members of the family, such as this mother, who mourn over these evil effects of sin?

They can find comfort in the hope that the Lord's saving power will bring healing to the family through their confident intercession. It comforts them to realize that those they are interceding for are brothers and sisters for whom Christ died, so they have reason to hope. Their prayers, made in unshakeable trust in God and love for the erring ones, bring comfort. Their confidence in God's infinite mercy and power brings consolation. They also find comfort in the courage they find as they pray.

Mourning over Other Evils

When one mourns over sin and its evil effects, consolation comes only when repentance removes this evil. But in the case of evils other than sin, for example, the death of a loved one, unemployment, or a serious illness such as cancer, one can find comfort even while the evil remains by trusting in

God, rejoicing in hope (cf. Rm 12:12). Trust in God makes patient endurance possible and easier. "We know that all things work together for good for those who love God" (Rm 8:28).

The comfort comes not only from hope of future glory, but from the courage and strength God gives us to deal with the suffering. The full meaning of the Greek word for comfort used in this beatitude makes this clear. The word translated as "comforted" can also be translated as "encouraged." The meaning depends on the context. As Jesus expresses it in this beatitude, "comforted" is the better word, because it refers both to the perfect consolation of heaven and to the comfort that comes from courage on earth.

St. Paul uses it in Second Corinthians, where it is best translated as "encouragement," because he is speaking of afflictions and sufferings to be endured now, in union with Christ. Paul's use of the word enlightens us about this. He speaks both of his and the Corinthians' sharing in Christ's suffering. Paul uses both the verb form *parakaleo* and the noun form *paraklesis*. Some translations render the words as "to console" and "consolation": "If we are being consoled, it is for your consolation" (2 Cor 1:6). But the context, speaking of present afflictions still to be endured, calls for the other meaning, "to encourage" and "encouragement," as in this translation:

> Blessed be the God and Father of our Lord Jesus Christ, the Father of compassion and God of all encouragement, who encourages us in our every affliction, so that we may be able to encourage those who are in any affliction with the encouragement with which we ourselves are encouraged by God. For as Christ's sufferings overflow to us, so through Christ does our encouragement also overflow. If we are afflicted, it is for your encouragement and salva-

> tion; if we are encouraged, it is for your encourage-
> ment, which enables you to endure the same suffer-
> ings that we suffer. Our hope for you is firm, for we
> know that as you share in the sufferings, you also
> share in the encouragement (2 Cor 1:3–7 NAB).

In this passage Paul repeats the words "affliction" and "suffering," hardships still to be endured, that call for encouragement. We might prefer that God console us by removing the afflictions. But we have not yet entered heaven. We are "joint heirs with Christ, if, in fact, we suffer with him so that we may also be glorified with him" (Rm 8:17).

Another translation of the above passage from Second Corinthians reads, "Just as the sufferings of Christ overflow into our lives, so does the encouragement we receive from Christ" (2 Cor 1:5 NJB). One finds encouragement from Christ when one sees sufferings as a sharing in Christ's sufferings. "If we receive encouragement," says Paul, "this is to gain for you the encouragement which enables you to bear with perseverance the same sufferings as we do" (2 Cor 1:6 NJB). We have solidarity with Christ and one another both in suffering and in encouragement. We suffer in community; we encourage one another in community.

"The sufferings of Christ overflow into our lives" (2 Cor 1:5 NJB). This can give us joy as well as courage. Joy in suffering becomes possible in fervent Christian life when we see our sufferings joined to Christ's. This gives them the redemptive value of the Lord's own sufferings.

"Blessed are those who mourn, for they shall be comforted." Who will comfort them? Why didn't Jesus say, "The Father will comfort them," or "I will console them," or "The Holy Spirit, the Paraclete, will encourage them"? "They shall be comforted" is a Jewish circumlocution to avoid using the deeply reverenced name of God. This occurs also in other beatitudes: "they will be filled," "they will receive mercy." Obviously God satisfies hunger and thirst for righteousness; God gives mercy to the merciful; God encourages and comforts those who mourn.

Paraclete, the name Jesus gave to the Holy Spirit (cf. Jn 14:26), usually translated as "Comforter" or "Advocate," could be translated as "Encourager." It is another form of the words *paraklesis* (encouragement) and *parakaleo* (to encourage.) By the gift of fortitude, the Holy Spirit forms courage and steadfast patience in the Christian, thus perfecting in that person the beatitudes of meekness and mourning. The Holy Spirit bestows the gift of fortitude upon us, patient endurance with Christ while we live on earth. To live the beatitude of consolation in mourning, one must invoke the Holy Spirit of fortitude, who empowers us to be patient in every sadness. That is why Aquinas teaches that the Spirit's gift of fortitude perfects the beatitudes of meekness and mourning in us (cf. *Summa Theol.*, I–II, q. 69, a. 2, *ad* 3).

"May the God of steadfastness and encouragement grant you to live in harmony with one another, in accordance with Christ Jesus, so that together you may with one voice glorify the God and Father of our Lord Jesus Christ" (Rm 15:5–6).

13

The Meek

Blessed are the meek,
for they will inherit the earth (Mt 5:5).

The Strength of the Meek

People do not like to be called meek, for meekness seems like weakness. But the virtue of meekness requires great strength of character. The dictionary defines meekness as "a mildness and patience of disposition, which is not easily stirred to anger or resentment."

Patience is a virtue, a strength. The word "virtue" comes from the Latin *vir,* man. The virtuous man or woman is strong, self-possessed, self-controlled, master of self and all one's powers. It takes a strong character to be patient in difficult situations, not easily moved to anger or resentment. Love "is not irritable or resentful" (1 Cor 13:5). It is a great work of mercy to bear wrongs patiently.

The dictionary definition of "patient" makes it clear that strong people show patience and meekness. Patient means "bearing or enduring pain, trouble, etc., without complaining or losing self-control or making a disturbance; refusing to be provoked or angered; forbearing, tolerant." Surely patience as self-possession shows strength.

Meekness is the virtue, the strength, that controls anger and resentment, whether toward God or others. "Meekness" has a strong, virile meaning. Unfortunately, it has also taken on a secondary meaning that causes people to forget its primary, strong meaning. The secondary meaning is "tamely submissive, easily imposed upon, too submissive, spineless, spiritless." This does not show virtue but weakness. Virtue does not submit weakly when one should stand up for what is right. Precisely because they stand up for the good, the disciples of Christ suffer persecution.

As a virtue, meekness stands midway between two extremes: uncontrolled anger and resentment on one hand, and on the other, weakly giving in, not responding to injustice or injury, not getting angry when one ought to. The truly meek person, the one who has the virtue, can display virtuous anger. At times it is right and just to show anger, as Jesus did on several occasions: Jesus "looked around at them with anger; he was grieved at their hardness of heart" (Mk 3:5). True meekness marks the morally strong, for it is the ability to control and use well the God-given power to get angry. Righteous anger can move a person, for example, to fight for social justice. Righteous anger inspired by hunger and thirst for justice can coexist with meekness, since the virtue of meekness helps us control anger and use it well.

Between the two extremes of uncontrolled, vengeful anger and spineless submission to injustice, a third way is sometimes called for, namely, patiently enduring injustice when it is inescapable. This requires great strength of character. It demands heroically controlling anger without spinelessly submitting to injustice. But how does one know when this patient endurance of wrong is called for? How does one know when not to defend self, as Jesus remained silent before his judges? When should one turn the other cheek? Difficult situations can arise, and in such cases a person may need to seek counsel. Certainly no one is required to submit to abusive treatment.

When Jesus said, "If anyone strikes you on the right cheek, turn the other also" (Mt 5:39), he was forbidding revenge. At times justice and right demand that we protest injustice, but this must always be done lovingly, without a vengeful spirit. It must be done in love's true concern for the salvation of the unjust one. "If your brother sins (against you), go and tell him his fault between you and him alone. If he listens to you, you have won over your brother" (Mt 18:15 NAB), you have saved him from harming himself by his sin. If the unjust one persists in injustice even though the injured one stands up for the right, and further objection to the injustice is fruitless, then it is better to endure it for the Lord's sake than to retaliate. This is to turn the other cheek.

Jesus, Meek and Humble of Heart (Mt 11:29)

Where do we learn the true meaning of the beatitude, "Blessed are the meek"? From Jesus who challenges us, "Learn from me, for I am meek and humble of heart" (Mt 11:29 NAB).

Throughout his Gospel, Matthew presents Jesus as the meek and humble suffering Servant of Yahweh. John protests when Jesus comes to the Jordan to be baptized, but Jesus replies, "Allow it now, for thus it is fitting for us to fulfill all righteousness" (Mt 3:15). Obedience to the Father fulfills righteousness. Jesus submits to baptism to signify his humble acceptance of the Father's will, and the Father responds, saying, "This is my beloved Son, with whom I am well pleased" (Mt 3:17). These words clearly echo the first servant poem of Isaiah, "Here is my servant whom I uphold, my chosen, in whom my soul delights; I have put my spirit upon him" (Is 42:1).

Thus at his baptism, Jesus is meek and humble of heart,

accepting his mission as the Servant sent to fulfill all righteousness. The Servant carries out his mission in meekness;
he is not vindictive, crushing the sinner; he does not
trample down the rebellious in anger: "A bruised reed he
will not break, and a dimly burning wick he will not
quench; he will faithfully bring forth justice" (Is 42:3).

When he met opposition, Jesus did not respond with
vengeful anger nor battle with his opponents. He quietly
withdrew from them and continued his mission of compassion and healing. Matthew states: "Many crowds followed
him, and he cured all of them.... This was to fulfill what had
been spoken through the prophet Isaiah: 'Here is my servant, whom I have chosen, my beloved, with whom my soul
is well pleased'" (Mt 12:15, 17–18). Matthew inserts the
word "beloved" into his quotation from Isaiah to remove
all doubt that Jesus is the Servant Isaiah described.

Jesus says to all of us, "Learn from me, for I am meek
and humble of heart." In other words, he expects humility
and meekness of all his disciples. These necessary virtues
help us to carry out our mission as God's servants, continu-
ing Jesus' mission as the suffering Servant of Yahweh.

The Richer Meaning of "Meek"

In joining meekness with humility, Jesus associates two
beatitudes, "Blessed are the poor in spirit" and "Blessed are
the meek."

The words, "Blessed are the meek, for they will inherit
the earth," derive from the Greek version of Psalm 37:11,
"The meek shall inherit the earth." In Hebrew, the words
are, "The *anawim* (the poor) shall inherit the earth." Why
was *anawim* (poor) translated into Greek by *praus* (meek)?
Is meekness the same as humility, the basic trait of the
anawim? Are the first and third beatitudes only two aspects
of the same reality?

To answer this, we need to understand the problem

faced by those who translated the Scriptures from Hebrew into Greek before the time of Christ. In Hebrew the words *anawim* and *anayyim* had taken on rich religious overtones, connoting the needy person's trust in God. But the corresponding Greek words for poverty, destitution and neediness had no such religious connotations, no suggestion of trust in God when troubles struck.

Fortunately the translators did find two Greek words having noble overtones: the adjective *praus* (meek), and the noun *prautes* (the meek). They often used these words in translating the Hebrew words for the poor and humble. Thus these translators, who knew their native Hebrew well, accurately interpreted for Greek readers the religious meaning of the Hebrew vocabulary of the *anawim*.

Praus means "gentle, unassuming, considerate, peaceful, peaceable toward others, merciful." *Prautes* means "gentleness, benevolence." Thus *praus* (meek) and *prautes* (meekness), mean much more than control of anger. Meekness as the virtue regulating anger is only part of a much larger personal disposition, not merely self-control, but gentleness, kindness and peaceableness toward others. In choosing these Greek words, the translators enriched the vocabulary of the *anawim*. For *praus* and *prautes* make explicit some of the meaning that was still hidden in the Hebrew words describing the *anawim*.

As we saw in treating the first beatitude, the *anawim* stood humbly before Yahweh in their neediness, "trembling at his word." They obeyed his *Torah*, well aware of their weakness and sinfulness, and always had childlike trust in their God.

A person living in such a relationship with God will inevitably acquire an inner peace, the fruit of trust in the Lord. This brings patient understanding of other people, gentle compassion and mercy toward them, an attitude of peacemaking. *Praus* and *prautes* as used by the translators explicitly expressed the gentleness and benevolence toward others that flow from humility toward God. The Greek *prautes* brought out what was implicit in the Hebrew word *anawah*, humility.

In presenting the beatitudes to us in Greek, the evangelist Matthew had a ready-made word, *praus*, to express more clearly both aspects of humility. It involves not only a relationship with God in trusting neediness, but a loving, patient, gentle relationship with other people. When Jesus says, "Learn from me, for I am meek and humble of heart," these two words express both aspects, humility and gentleness toward God and neighbor. Gentleness toward others comes with true humility. Truly, the beatitude of the meek brings out another aspect of the humility of the poor in spirit.

Jesus Described As Praus *(Meek)*

The way Matthew uses the word *praus* in speaking of Jesus helps us appreciate the full richness of the beatitude, "Blessed are the meek." Matthew uses *praus* to express Jesus' humble acceptance of his lowly condition as the Servant of Yahweh. Though the word does not occur the first time that Matthew presents Jesus as the Servant (at his baptism by John), Matthew later uses the word in speaking of Jesus as Servant, showing that it applies here, also.

Repeatedly in his Gospel, Matthew underlines Jesus' meekness, but above all in the account of his passion. Our Lord comes to Jerusalem to face insults, abuse, rejection, scourging, mockery and death on the cross. He comes meek *(praus)*, riding on a lowly ass (cf. Mt 21:1–11), humbly accepting his mission as suffering Servant.

But he comes in zeal for justice, protesting evil. Immediately after he enters the city in meekness and humility, anger inflames him as he drives the moneychangers from the temple, protesting the greed which has turned the house of prayer into a den of thieves (cf. Mt 21:12–13). Thus he shows that meekness and righteous anger can indeed coexist in the same person.

Three times Jesus had foretold the horrible treatment he would receive in Jerusalem for standing up for what was right. The third time he spoke of this, he was already on the way to face it. Certainly Jesus, meek and humble of heart, showed courage and fortitude all the way up to Jerusalem. He accepted the cross in obedience to the Father. At the same time he had no resentment or hatred for those who would kill him. In describing our Lord's entry into Jerusalem, Matthew highlights Jesus' meekness by quoting the prophet Zechariah:

> "Tell the daughter of Zion,
> Look, your king is coming to you,
> humble, and mounted on a donkey" (Mt 21:5).

According to Zechariah, the messiah would come to Jerusalem as a peacemaker, not as a conquering warrior. He expresses his peaceful intent by coming in humility, not on a battle horse, but on a lowly donkey.

Jesus the messiah is a peacemaker, and shows the way for those to whom he says, "Blessed are the peacemakers, for they will be called children of God" (Mt 5:9). His meekness as he enters Jerusalem shows his peaceful intent. He did not come with an army on war horses to conquer a temporal kingdom. He comes with gentleness and compassion, "*praus* and riding on an ass."

As he enters the city Jesus knows that he will meet opposition, persecution, rejection and death, but he does not retaliate in anger. He shows the way for his disciples, to whom he says, "Blessed are those who are persecuted for righteousness' sake, for theirs is the kingdom of heaven" (Mt 5:10). He lived the beatitudes which he presents to us.

Even if his disciples are persecuted for their zeal for

justice, Jesus tells them not to exhibit a vengeful spirit, but to forgive. He tells them not to "get even," to try to set things right by doing another wrong. "Human anger does not produce God's righteousness" (Jas 1:20).

Christ shows meekness by quietly accepting, in patient humility, the difficult mission the Father gave him. He did not complain or resent his Father. Jesus' meekness implies great strength of character as he carries out his God-given mission. He accepts the Father's will without anger or rebellion. His actions reflect the suffering Servant Isaiah described:

> The Lord God has opened my ear,
>   and I was not rebellious,
>   I did not turn backward.
> I gave my back to those who struck me,
>   and my cheeks to those who pulled out the
>   beard.
> I did not hide my face from insult and spitting
>   (Is 50:5–6).

His meekness calls for courageous obedience to his Father, and loving gentleness toward those who reject and crucify him. He has protested against evil to no avail; further words would fall on deaf ears. So in humble silence he accepts the cup of suffering, with no revenge toward his persecutors.

Yet by his willingness to suffer he protests most eloquently against injustice. Jesus practiced the eighth beatitude; he suffered persecution for righteousness' sake (Mt 5:10). Had he drawn back in fear of suffering and ceased protesting injustice, this would have been false meekness. But Jesus' burning zeal for the Father's glory empowered him with love's willingness and courage to suffer for what is right. "Zeal for your house will consume me" (Jn 2:17; cf. Ps 69:9).

Jesus' entry into Jerusalem, "meek and riding on an ass," sets the scene for his passion and death. It describes how Jesus acts throughout his passion. He is the humble and lowly king Matthew described: "They stripped him and put a scarlet robe on him, and after twisting some thorns into a crown, they put it on his head. They put a reed in his right hand and knelt before him and mocked him, saying, 'Hail, King of the Jews!'" (Mt 27:28–29).

Through it all, Jesus remains silent. He speaks no word of anger or resentment, utters no threat of vengeance, displays no bitterness over his hard lot in life. "He committed no sin, and no deceit was found in his mouth. When he was abused, he did not return abuse; when he suffered he did not threaten, but he entrusted himself to the one who judges justly.... By his wounds you have been healed" (1 Pet 2:22–24). He accepts all as his Father's will, meek and humble to the end, strong in his self-possession. Meekness does not mean weakness.

Learn from Me

Jesus declares so firmly, "Blessed are the meek, for they will inherit the earth" (Mt 5:5). Jesus challenges us, "Learn from me, for I am meek and humble of heart" (Mt 11:29 NAB). His own example in carrying his cross lightens our burden. For when we carry it as he carried his, without hatred or resentment, as a servant who lovingly obeys the Father, we can carry our burden more easily. It frees us from the added, galling burden of resisting God's will:

"Come to me, all you that are weary and are carrying heavy burdens, and I will give you rest. Take my yoke upon you, and learn from me, for I am gentle and humble in heart, and you will find rest for your souls. For my yoke is easy, and my burden is light" (Mt 11:28–30).

We take upon ourselves the yoke of our Lord's teachings, all he has commanded. This yoke does burden us, for his teachings demand sacrifice. Yet this yoke is easy and this burden light, because we learn from the Lord's meekness and humility how to accept it. We can imitate his humble, loving obedience to the Father, his zeal for the Father's glory.

We learn from Jesus how to take up the yoke of obedience to his word. We learn this not only from contemplating him as he steadfastly goes up to Jerusalem to suffer. We see this courageous acceptance of the Father's will from the beginning of his redeeming work. The patience he showed while his tormentors mocked and scourged and crucified him did not begin then. He showed this same humble acceptance from the day he began his public life when John baptized him, calling Jesus the Lamb of God. Indeed, Jesus showed it from the instant of his incarnation: "When Christ came into the world, he said...'I have come to do your will, O God'" (Heb 10:5, 7). He showed it again when he said to Mary and Joseph when they found him in the temple, "Did you not know that I must be in my Father's house?" (Lk 2:49).

Clearly, the example of Jesus, whom Matthew repeatedly describes as *praus* (meek), shows that meekness is far more than the virtue that regulates anger. Meekness requires a complete self-possession that is humbly obedient to God, gentle, peaceful and that does good to neighbor. It never asserts self at the expense of others. Whoever has learned all this from Jesus truly lives the blessedness of this beatitude even on earth. The self-possessed, those who are strong enough to rule themselves, inherit the earth and govern it well.

"They Will Inherit the Earth"

What does it mean to say that the meek "will inherit the earth"? Does it mean that even now on earth we can enjoy the blessedness won by meekness?

Psalm 37:11 states that "the meek shall inherit *the land*." The Hebrew word *erets* can mean either the whole earth or a particular land, depending on the context. When it refers to the land God promised to Abraham and his descendants, it is translated as "the land," as in Psalm 37.

Did God specify conditions for possessing the promised land? Yes. Along with meekness, Psalm 37 lists various characteristics of those who will inherit it. "The meek *(anawim)* shall inherit the land" (v. 11). "The *righteous* shall inherit the land and live in it forever" (v. 29). "Trust in the Lord, and do good; so you will live in the land, and enjoy security" (v. 3). "Those who wait for the Lord shall inherit the land" (v. 9). "Those blessed by the Lord shall inherit the land" (v. 22). "Wait for the Lord, and keep to his way, and he will exalt you to inherit the land" (v. 34).

The *anawim* have all these qualities. As the righteous, they walk in the Lord's way and trust in him with humility and gentleness. They lovingly give others their just due, mercifully responding to their needs.

In Deuteronomy, the Lord insists that only the just will possess the land. "Justice, and only justice, you shall pursue, so that you may live and occupy the land that the Lord your God is giving you" (Dt 16:20). To possess the land in peace and security requires that God's people deal justly with one another. But the fullness of justice exists only with mercy and meekness.

When Jesus quotes Psalm 37:11, saying, "Blessed are the meek, for they will possess the earth," obviously he does not mean that piece of land promised to Abraham, for Jesus' disciples live all over the earth. He commanded them, "Go therefore and make disciples of all nations" (Mt 28:19).

"Blessed are the meek, for they will inherit the earth," we have seen, is another facet of the beatitude, "Blessed are the poor in spirit, for theirs is the kingdom of heaven." Thus "they will inherit the earth" is another way of saying "the kingdom of heaven is theirs." But "the kingdom of heaven" is a reverential circumlocution for "the kingdom of God." Though the kingdom will be completely established only in the next life, it begins here on earth. We will understand what it means to inherit the earth when we understand what the kingdom of God is in its beginnings on earth.

To Enjoy Peace Is to Possess the Land

The metaphor "the kingdom of God" expresses all the blessings of salvation, all the blessings the messiah brings. The word *shalom* (peace) sums up these blessings. Psalm 37:11 states that to inherit the land is to enjoy abundant and undisturbed peace: "The humble *(anawim)* will possess the land and will taste the delights of an unfathomable peace *(shalom)*" (Ps 37:11; cf. LEON-DUFOUR, p. 412).

This sentence has typical Hebrew parallelism; a statement is made, then restated in other words. "Taste the delights of an unfathomable peace" is a more explicit way of saying "possess the land." The meek will possess the land. True peace will reign only when meekness reigns in the hearts and lives of the people. Peace flows from meekness, for meekness is an integral element of *anawah,* the humility of the *anawim*. The righteousness required for possessing the land calls for humility and meekness.

The Hebrew word *shalom* (peace), has taken on such richness of meaning that no one English word can express it. It derives from a root word meaning intact, whole, complete. As wholeness, *shalom* is the well-being of people who live in harmony with nature, with themselves, with one another, and with God. It includes security, freedom from fear, and concord in a life of true brotherly and sisterly *ḥesed*.

Although *shalom* is often rendered as "prosperity," this translation does not express all its aspects, because in English "prosperity" mainly connotes material wealth. For biblical people, *shalom* did have a material dimension, yet it also speaks of well-being on every level of life: material, moral and spiritual. It includes moral integrity (righteousness) and therefore good order within a person, and in relation to others and to God. Because it concerns right relationships with others, it is the fruit of justice: "Then justice will dwell in the wilderness, and righteousness abide in the fruitful field. *The effect of righteousness will be peace,* and the result of righteousness, quietness and trust forever" (Is 32:16–17). The peace of God's reign will bring these blessings. Only justice eliminates sin, the source of divisions, warfare, fear, insecurity and lack of trust. Full justice flows from humility and meekness, while much injustice stems from pride and aggression. Only Yahweh can bring the blessing of peace into sinful human life: "Let me hear what God the Lord will speak, for he will speak peace to his people, to his faithful, to those who turn to him in their hearts" (Ps 85:8).

Shalom flows from God's reign of justice. As the "prince of peace," the messiah will give "endless peace" (Is 9:6–7). "He shall be the one of peace" (Micah 5:5).

Psalm 37 is like a meditation on this promise of *shalom.* The righteous, those who keep the Lord's way, will inherit the land. Only those who do justice in meekness will occupy the land in security and overflowing peace.

Yet one might ask, "When Psalm 37 was composed (most likely after Israel's return from exile in Babylon), did not God's people again possess the land promised to Abraham? Why does the psalm say at least six times, 'They shall inherit the land'?"

As the fruit of the righteousness that alone brings security, *shalom* goes beyond mere physical presence in the land. One does not really possess the land if one faces the perpetual danger of being cheated out of it or dispossessed by tyrants, creditors, or foreign invaders.

In a remarkable passage, the Book of Leviticus describes *shalom* as peace and fullness on every level of life, including many children, good harvests, security from enemies, peace with neighbors, God's presence with his people: "If you... keep my commandments...the land shall yield its produce.... You shall eat your bread to the full, and live securely in your land. And I will grant peace in the land, and you shall lie down, and no one shall make you afraid...no sword shall go through your land.... I will look with favor upon you and make you fruitful and multiply you.... And I will walk among you, and will be your God, and you shall be my people" (Lev 26:3–13).

Surely all these thoughts are packed into that statement of Jesus, "Blessed are the meek, for they will inherit the land." His words refer to psalm 37:11, "The meek shall inherit the land, and taste the delights of an unfathomable peace."

Is all this an impossible ideal? Can one hope to "inherit the earth" in a war-ridden time like ours with its ongoing threats of terrorism? Or does the beatitude refer only to the next life, to heaven? What elements of *shalom* can the meek enjoy even now? What ways of the meek will produce peace? To answer these questions, let us again consider meekness and humility, especially as integral elements of righteousness.

The Self-Possessed Possess the Land

Righteousness, the condition for possessing the land in peace, involves right relationships among a whole people. But it presupposes the personal righteousness of the individuals who make up that people. When injustice plagues the whole earth, or a nation, city or smaller community, no one enjoys peace and security. Thieves, vandals and terrorists threaten to destroy material goods, while worry and fear destroy peace of mind.

Yet even then, to the extent that individuals or groups practice meekness, they will have a degree of *shalom* and will "possess the land." First, they will enjoy the interior personal peace that results from self-possession. To that degree, they will "possess the earth" and foster peace in their community.

Disputes and injustices in human society spring from disorder in the human heart. St. James states this very clearly: "Those conflicts and disputes among you, where do they come from? Do they not come from your cravings that are at war within you? You want something and do not have it; so you commit murder. And you covet something, and cannot obtain it, so you engage in disputes and conflicts..." (Jas 4:1–3). Wars begin in the human heart.

Self-possession remedies this warfare within a person. First of all, a person must possess "the land" of self. The various virtues that bring about self-possession come under "meekness" in its broad sense as self-control. In the narrow dictionary sense, meekness means control of the passions that give rise to anger, resentment and vengeance. But commenting on "the meek shall possess the earth," Thomas Aquinas broadens it to include control of all the emotional powers. Meekness is then equivalent to self-control, self-possession.

Aquinas expresses all this in a dense sentence that sums up his teaching on self-possession: "The possession of the land denotes the well-ordered affections of the soul, which rests, in desire, on the solid foundation of the eternal inheritance" (*Summa Theol.*, I–II, q. 69, a. 2, *ad* 3). When the heart desires God in love and hope, and turns every desire and affection toward God, then that person "possesses the land" in the sense of self-possession, and directs every thought, desire and action toward God, the true inheritance.

Thus to possess the land, one must possess self by

regulating anger and violence with patience and meekness, sexual desire with chastity, ambition and lust for power with humility, the desire for food with temperance, and so on. That is what Aquinas means in saying that possessing the land, even now on earth, consists in rightly ordering the affections toward God.

The self-possessed, guiding all their affections, can master themselves and not let passions such as lust, greed and ambition dominate them. For example, the desire for money and wealth dominates the avaricious person, but the self-possessed person can freely use material things as their master, not their slave. "All things are yours.... All belong to you, and you belong to Christ, and Christ belongs to God" (1 Cor 3:21–22). When, in Christ, we give our hearts and lives to God, we can regulate our desires and use all things well in the service of God. This is to "possess the land" even now, and not let it possess us.

All this fits in well with Psalm 37, which speaks of "righteousness," "meekness" and "walking in the way of the Lord" as different aspects of the same reality, like facets of a diamond. It also fits in well with what St. James wrote about meekness as humble self-possession:

> Show by your good life that your works are done with gentleness *(prautes)* born of wisdom. But if you have bitter envy and selfish ambition in your hearts, do not be boastful and false to the truth. Such wisdom does not come down from above, but is earthly, unspiritual, devilish. For where there is envy and selfish ambition, there will also be disorder and wickedness of every kind. But the wisdom from above is first pure, then peaceable, gentle, *willing to yield,* full of mercy and good fruits, without a trace of partiality or hypocrisy. And a harvest of righteousness is sown in peace for those who make peace (Jas 3:13–18).

The words "willing to yield" are italicized above because they express the essence of meekness. The meek have yielded their rights to God and have not taken them back. They desire to give God full liberty to do with them what he wills. This is the meekness of Jesus who said, "My Father, if it is possible, let this cup pass from me; yet not what I want but what you want" (Mt 26:39), and, "Father, into your hands I commend my spirit" (Lk 23:46). The meek are "willing to yield" to others, "turning the other cheek" for the Lord's sake, rather than seeking revenge.

Sins against Meekness

We sin against the beatitude of meekness not only by uncontrolled anger, but also by dominating others (James calls it "selfish ambition"—Jas 3:14, 16). This includes controlling others rather than serving them, being insensitive and harsh, considering ourselves better than others, and putting our needs before theirs.

St. Paul presents Jesus' meekness and humility as a model for ours. He describes how we can practice these virtues, and shows them to us in the person of Jesus:

> Do nothing from selfish ambition or conceit, but in humility regard others as better than yourselves. Let each of you look not to your own interests, but to the interests of others. Let the same mind be in you that was in Christ Jesus, who though he was in the form of God, did not regard equality with God as something to be exploited, but emptied himself, taking the form of a slave, being born in human likeness. And being found in human form, he humbled himself and became obedient to the point of death—even death on a cross (Phil 2:3–8).

Paul paints this picture of the meek and humble Jesus to illustrate what he had just said about meekness, humility and serving others. What good is it to admire these virtues in Jesus if we do not live them ourselves?

To the extent that we live the Paschal Mystery in humble obedience and service, we share in the power of the risen Lord to win the world for God. We possess the earth to the degree that we conquer the earth for Christ, sharing in his mission. But we can do this only in the degree that we share in the meekness and humility of the suffering Servant.

14

The Righteous

Blessed are those who hunger and thirst
for righteousness, for they will be filled (Mt 5:6).

"With Righteousness He Shall Judge the Poor"

"Blessed are those who hunger and thirst for righteousness,
for they shall be filled" (Mt 5:6).

In this beatitude we again find Yahweh's poor ones, this
time as victims of injustice. Oppressed, deprived of their
rights, they ask God to vindicate them: "How long must
your servant endure? When will you judge those who persecute me?" (Ps 119:84).

Again and again in the Bible, the poor and oppressed
call out to God for help. The crimes committed against
them cry out to heaven for justice. After Cain murdered his
brother Abel, God reproached him, "Listen, your brother's
blood is crying out to me from the ground!" (Gen 4:10).
Speaking to Moses from the burning bush, Yahweh said,
"The cry of the Israelites has now come to me; I have also
seen how the Egyptians oppress them" (Ex 3:9).

Every injustice people inflict on others affronts the just
God and outrages his holiness. It disturbs the order of
justice he has established for his creatures. God must vindi-

cate his justice by setting things right. Injustice also deeply distresses God's friends. In zeal for God's glory, they hunger and thirst for his justice that will set things right.

Isaiah says much about this. He declares that God's holiness will shine forth when his righteousness judges the unjust and restores justice: "The Lord of hosts is exalted by justice, and the Holy God shows himself holy by righteousness" (Is 5:16). God's righteous action manifests his holiness.

His people's hunger and thirst for righteousness show zeal for the holiness of God, a concern for his glory. Their outrage at the injustices in the world around them signifies their holiness. Affronts to God's holiness deeply pain the psalmist, who says to the Lord, "It is zeal for your house that has consumed me; the insults of those who insult you have fallen on me" (Ps 69:9). Distressed by the injustices he saw among those buying and selling in the temple, Jesus protested, "Is it not written, 'My house shall be called a house of prayer for all the nations'? But you have made it a den of robbers" (Mk 11:17). Zealous for justice and holiness, he made a whip and drove out the money changers, along with their sheep and cattle. Clearly, Jesus experienced hunger and thirst for righteousness. Injustice always pained him.

The beatitude of meekness does not submit to injustice. When God's people protest injustices and work to rectify them, they provoke persecution, and courageously suffer it for the sake of righteousness. They do not fight injustice out of revenge, but with zeal for the holiness of God and the rights of the oppressed. Their just anger works patiently, with the strength of meekness, to vindicate the rights of all.

Zeal for justice necessarily involves protesting injustice. Jesus himself protested when the high priest's servant unjustly struck him on the cheek (cf. Jn 18:22–23). St. Paul did the same (cf. Acts 23:2–3), protesting when the civil authorities violated his rights as a Roman citizen (cf. Acts 16:37; 22:25). Virtue protests against injustice, for the virtue of justice directs us to act zealously for God. Every injustice offends God's glory and holiness, so God's people work zealously for social justice.

Sometimes silent endurance of persecution, as Jesus remained silent before Caiaphas, protests most eloquently against injustice. Jesus had spoken out in his public ministry and provoked persecution. His silent endurance of persecution crowned his zeal for righteousness.

The cries of the poor and oppressed fill the psalms as they ask for justice from God. "Vindicate me, O Lord, my God, according to your righteousness, and do not let them rejoice over me" (Ps 35:24). God complains that injustice dishonors him: "How long, you people, shall my honor suffer shame?" (Ps 4:2).

God expects human judges to act justly. He calls them to account in his own court of justice: "God has taken his place in the divine council; in the midst of the gods he holds judgment: 'How long will you judge unjustly and show partiality to the wicked? Give justice to the weak and the orphan; maintain the right of the lowly and the destitute. Rescue the weak and the needy; deliver them from the hand of the wicked'" (Ps 82:1–4). Not only judges, but also legislators, rulers and voters ought to take these words to heart. God's holiness demands justice in human government.

The Messiah: the Hope of the Oppressed

In their longing for justice, the oppressed poor of Yahweh longed for the coming of the messiah. Justice would characterize messianic times. Jeremiah announced that the messiah would be a righteous branch for David and his name would be "the Lord is our righteousness" (Jer 23:5–6). He would establish righteousness in his people. Isaiah calls him

Emmanuel (God with us), and declares, "with righteousness he shall judge the poor, and decide with equity for the
meek of the earth" (Is 11:4).

The suffering Servant of Yahweh, one of his poor ones,
hungers and thirsts for righteousness from God, entrusting
his cause to him. He possesses all the traits of Yahweh's
poor ones who hope in the Lord. Like his oppressed fellows,
the Servant asks God to vindicate him when the people he
tried to console reject and persecute him:

> The Lord God has given me the tongue of a
>   teacher,
>   that I may know how to sustain the weary with a
>   word.
> Morning by morning he wakens—
>   wakens my ear to listen as those who are taught.
> The Lord God has opened my ear,
>   and I was not rebellious, I did not turn
>   backward.
> I gave my back to those who struck me,
>   and my cheeks to those who pulled out the
>   beard;
> I did not hide my face from insult and spitting.
> The Lord God helps me;
>   therefore I have not been disgraced;
> therefore I have set my face like flint,
>   and I know that I shall not be put to shame;
>   *he who vindicates me is near.*
> Who will contend with me? Let us stand up
>   together.
>   Who are my adversaries? Let them confront me.
> It is the Lord God who helps me;
>   who will declare me guilty? (Is 50:4–9).

Like the suffering Servant, Jesus expects God to vindicate him. This will happen when the Holy Spirit comes. The
Spirit will manifest him as the Just One: "And when he

comes, he will prove the world wrong about sin and righteousness and judgment: about sin, because they do not believe in me; about righteousness, because I am going to the Father and you will see me no longer; about judgment, because the ruler of this world has been condemned" (Jn 16:8–11).

Jesus' vindication in his exaltation and sending of the Holy Spirit thus becomes the hope of all those who hunger and thirst for justice. In Christ's vindication, justice comes to all who remain faithful to him.

Though they do not see justice fully established here on earth, those who hunger and thirst for justice find beatitude even now, knowing that God's justice will prevail. They have the peace of knowing that "all things work together for good for those who love God" (Rm 8:28). With the hope that cannot be disappointed (cf. Rm 5:5), they trust that at the appointed time God will set all things right. The Lord's promise sustains them: "Blessed are those who hunger and thirst for righteousness, for they will be filled" (Mt 5:6).

They do not harbor bitter distress or rebel against their lot in life, even as they strive to improve it. In humility and gentle meekness they accept the truth that their loving Father in heaven holds all things in his hands. He orders everything for the good of those who love him. Just as he vindicated Jesus his Son when he was unjustly condemned, he will vindicate us too.

Hunger and Thirst for Justification

Righteousness has many aspects. God is righteous, and he forms righteousness in us. It includes justice in our relationships, righting wrongs done by injustice. Yahweh's poor hungered and thirsted for this righting of wrongs.

But they also hungered and thirsted for something more fundamental: their personal interior righteousness. They ardently longed for their personal justification, being right with God. The work of the messiah would accomplish this too. "The days are surely coming, says the Lord, when I will raise up for David a righteous Branch, and he shall reign as king and deal wisely, and shall execute justice and righteousness in the land.... And this is the name by which *he* will be called: 'The Lord is our righteousness'" (Jer 23:5–6). Jeremiah later repeats these words, but ends them by saying, "And this is the name by which *it* [Jerusalem] will be called, 'The Lord is our righteousness'" (Jer 33:14–16). The messiah's own name will be given to the people, signifying that he has formed his own righteousness in them.

In a passage from Micah, we see mourning Jerusalem longing for both elements of righteousness, and confidently expecting the Lord to bring them about in her. "Do not rejoice over me, O my enemy; when I fall, I shall rise; when I sit in darkness, the Lord will be a light to me. I must bear the indignation of the Lord, because I have sinned against him, until he takes my side and executes judgment for me. He will bring me out to the light; I shall see his vindication" (Micah 7:8–9).

Jerusalem mourns for her sins, figuratively sitting in sackcloth and ashes, and patiently endures the injustices her enemy has inflicted on her. This purifies her and sets her right with God, bringing about her interior justification. The prophet says to God, "You will cast all our sins into the depths of the sea" (Micah 7:19). God also vindicates her against her enemy.

In the last line of the passage from Micah quoted above, the phrase "I shall see his vindication" has been variously translated: "I will see his justice" (NAB), "I shall see his righteousness" (KJV), "I shall see his deliverance" (RSV). The Hebrew word can be translated accurately in these various ways because, as used here, it refers to God's righteousness in dealing with his creatures. It speaks both of God's righteous action and its effects on us. His righteous action breaks the chains that bind the oppressed and secures justice for them. Thus the word can be translated as "vindication" or "deliverance." But since it is God's work in us producing this effect, it is "his righteousness."

His righteousness produces different effects in us according to our different needs. It secures justice for the innocent and persecuted. It justifies sinners who appeal to his mercy. It satisfies those who hunger and thirst for holiness.

The passage from Micah will help us in reading what St. Paul says about justification in his letter to the Romans. He shows that God communicates his righteousness to us to make us righteous. God gives it to us in the grace of justification:

> But now, apart from law, the righteousness of God has been disclosed...the righteousness of God through faith in Christ for all who believe. For there is no distinction, since all have sinned and fall short of the glory of God; they are now justified by his grace as a gift, through the redemption that is in Christ Jesus, whom God put forward as a sacrifice of atonement by his blood, effective through faith. He did this to show *his righteousness,* because in his divine forbearance he had passed over the sins previously committed; it was to prove at the present time that *he himself is righteous* and that *he justifies* the one who has faith in Jesus (Rm 3:21–26).

God gives this gift of justification as the fruit of Christ's righteousness in doing the Father's will: "By the one man's obedience, the many will be made righteous" (Rm 5:19). He gives it to us by outpouring the Holy Spirit, who establishes us in righteousness by bringing us into Christ's own obedient relationship with the Father: "God has sent the Spirit of his Son into our hearts, crying, 'Abba! Father!'" (Gal 4:6).

Jesus alone can satisfy our hunger and thirst for righ-

teousness. Knowing their sinfulness, the poor and contrite
hunger and thirst for righteousness, even more than a no-
mad trudging under the desert sun thirsts for water. God
fills them with the interior personal rightness called the
grace of justification.

By this grace, Jesus establishes them in his obedience to
the Father, so that with him they cry out, "Abba, Father...
not what I want, but what you want" (Mk 14:36). Aquinas
writes, "Even in this life those who hunger and thirst for
righteousness can have their fill of that food of which our
Lord said, 'My food is to do the will of him who sent me'
(Jn 4:34)" (*Summa Theol.*, I–II, q. 69, a. 2, *ad* 3).

Aquinas attributes to the Holy Spirit's gift of piety the
beatitude, "Blessed are those who hunger and thirst for
righteousness, for they will be filled." When the Holy Spirit
forms in our hearts the Son's loving filial relationship with
the Father, he puts us right with God. The Spirit justifies us
and satisfies our hunger and thirst for righteousness.

The grace of justification is destined to grow into the
glory of heavenly fulfillment: "Those whom he called he
also justified; and those whom he justified he also glorified"
(Rm 8:30). Living in the grace of God gives us initial
beatitude. It pledges the eternal beatitude of glory. By our
hunger and thirst for righteousness, we ardently desire to
grow in holiness, deepening our loving relationship with
God our Father. "Not that I have already obtained this or
have already reached the goal," but hungering and thirsting
to possess it ever more securely and completely, "I press on
to make it my own, because Jesus Christ has made me his
own" (Phil 3:12).

Jesus enables us to share in his obedience, so that we do
everything in obedience to the Father. That Jesus may
accomplish this work in us, we yield ourselves to him in
faith's wholehearted *fiat:* "Be it done to me according to
your will." Our will then becomes one with his will.

St. Paul asks God to give us this perfect obedience, this living in the divine will: "And this is my prayer, that your love may overflow more and more with knowledge and full insight to help you to determine what is best, so that in the day of Christ you may be pure and blameless, having produced the harvest of righteousness that comes through Jesus Christ for the glory and praise of God" (Phil 1:9–11).

Poverty of spirit, humbly knowing that we can fall out of righteousness, leads to a hunger and thirst that only Jesus can satisfy. God blesses those who hunger and thirst for righteousness, because Jesus dwells in them to satisfy this desire.

The Righteousness

Jesus said, "Blessed are those who hunger and thirst for *the* righteousness" (Mt 5:6). The Greek of Matthew's Gospel uses the definite article "the" to indicate that Jesus speaks of a special kind of righteousness.

The Hebrew word meaning "righteous" originally had a juridical meaning. Only a qualified judge in a court could pronounce a person righteous or unrighteous. Biblical people realized that God alone, "the Judge of all the earth" (Gen 18:25), could judge their moral and religious righteousness, for he alone reads hearts.

When God made his covenant with his people, "righteousness" came to mean fidelity to the covenant, which specified the terms of moral and religious righteousness. Each person was judged according to the law of the covenant.

Jesus took this concept and enriched it. The righteousness he requires is an *abounding, overflowing fullness of merciful love* that Jesus calls *the* righteousness. The last judgment scene in Matthew's Gospel casts light on how we should understand it (cf. Mt 25:31–46). It tells us who God judges as righteous. The scene shows that the righteousness that obtains admission to the kingdom showers love and mercy on the needy: "I was hungry and you gave me food, I was thirsty and you gave me something to drink, I was a stranger and you welcomed me, I was naked and you gave me clothing, I was sick and you took care of me, I was in prison and you visited me" (Mt 25:35–36).

"Then the *righteous* will answer him, 'Lord, when was it that we saw you hungry and gave you food?...'" (Mt 25:37). Here the disciples are called righteous for the first time—only after the Judge has declared them such. During his days among them, Jesus had never called his disciples righteous. Up to the time of the judgment, they are not called righteous, but disciples. "Disciple" means "one who learns from a teacher." From Jesus, in humility, we still need to learn the ways of overflowing righteousness and to hunger and thirst for its fullness. We do not presume to call ourselves righteous, for we would sin by self-righteousness, a sin against poverty of spirit.

The righteousness of the kingdom is *mercy*—the generous love and compassion that cares for the poor and needy, and zealously defends their right to share in the world's resources.

In the Sermon on the Mount Jesus explains other elements of that abounding righteousness, that compassionate love that flows from mercy. He presents several examples of that overflowing love, inviting us to an abounding righteousness. For example, he taught, "You have heard that it was said, 'You shall love your neighbor and hate your enemy.' But I say to you, Love your enemies and pray for those who persecute you" (Mt 5:43–44). Mercy performs its supreme work by forgiving one's enemies.

Our Lord shows that the abounding righteousness consists in a fullness of love. Love not only avoids murder, but it controls anger, showing the beatitude of meekness (cf. Mt 5:21–22). It not only shuns adultery, but with purity of heart it guards even interior desires (cf. Mt 5:27–28). It always makes peace and seeks reconciliation with brother or sister: "Leave your gift there before the altar and go; first be reconciled to your brother or sister, and then come and offer your gift" (Mt 5:24).

Thus Jesus describes how we should act so as to enter the kingdom. If we show mercy and compassionate love, dealing justly with all, we will enter eternal life. Love cannot exist without justice. Compassion for the down and out is not enough. Full righteousness would not let anyone fall down and out in the first place. If we had a truly just social order, no one would go hungry and homeless and naked.

Righteousness, a Community Virtue

In the Old Testament, the terms "righteousness" and "mercy" (ḥesed) indicate the same thing. Righteousness means faithfulness to the covenant, a covenant of ḥesed. Yahweh, "the faithful God," keeps "covenant and mercy," that is, "his merciful covenant" (Dt 7:9 NAB). In making this covenant, he bound himself to show mercy to his people forever. By entering this covenant with Yahweh, the people bound themselves to "keep covenant and mercy" toward God and one another. They too had to show compassion and mercy. Since righteousness means fidelity to the covenant, the righteous person "keeps covenant and mercy," doing mercy toward all the members of the covenant.

Righteousness by its nature involves a relationship. It means being right with God and right with one another in the covenant community. As a relationship it is a community virtue. It concerns not only each one's individual righteousness, but that of the whole group. It results in community living and builds up the body of Christ. By it, we are "united in love.... The whole body, nourished and held together by its ligaments and sinews, grows with a growth that is from God" (Col 2:2, 19).

The kingdom of God consists in the overflowing righteousness Jesus requires. "Strive first for the kingdom of God and his righteousness, and all these things will be given to you as well" (Mt 6:33). In this saying of Jesus, "righteousness" is another word for "kingdom." Where righteousness reigns, God reigns in the hearts and lives of his people, governed by his holy will. "The kingdom of God is not food and drink, but righteousness and peace and joy in the Holy Spirit" (Rm 14:17). As right community relationship in merciful love, righteousness makes for peace, unity and joy. Jesus sent the Holy Spirit to work these things in us.

We express our hunger and thirst for merciful righteousness each time we pray in the Lord's Prayer, "Your kingdom come, your will be done" (Mt 6:10). The kingdom comes to the extent that we live according to God's will. We can do this only by the grace of the Holy Spirit, given to us as the fruit of Jesus' sacrificial obedience on the cross to the will of God. God wills that we keep the covenant of mercy he has sealed with us in the blood of his Son Jesus.

Obviously, hunger for righteousness longs for more than one's personal right relationship with God. It longs for the holiness of the whole Christian community of God's people, and indeed for that of the whole community of nations. It ardently desires the rightness of all human society, what recent Popes have called "a civilization of love." For it is "the mystery of his will...to gather up all things in him [Christ], things in heaven and things on earth" (Eph 1:9).

We hunger and thirst for righteousness because as individuals and as a people, we do not yet fully possess it. We hunger and thirst for it because we see that the world about us still lacks it. Sin abounds in the world; even our Christian community falls short. The injustices all around us deeply distress us.

Therefore we hunger and thirst for the righteousness of

the whole world. We hunger and thirst for it especially because we know that we ourselves so often fail. We pray for it and mourn over our unrighteousness. In humility, poverty of spirit, we do not declare ourselves righteous, knowing that God alone can judge us.

Hunger and thirst for community righteousness expresses itself in many other ways. In solidarity with those who suffer, God asks us to mourn with those who mourn, do penance for those who sin, lovingly work to win back our brothers and sisters who have sinned against us (cf. Mt 18:15). God asks us to show gentleness toward all, bear no resentments, hold no grudges and nourish no hatred, for all these destroy community. In humility, we act as Paul urged: "Do nothing from selfish ambition or conceit, but in humility regard others as better than yourselves. Let each of you look not to your own interests, but to the interests of others" (Phil 2:3–4).

If we do all these things, God will satisfy more and more our hunger and thirst for righteousness. Even now on earth, we will enjoy this beatitude to the extent that we live in this merciful righteousness, in the peace and joy of the indwelling Holy Spirit.

"To Fulfill All Righteousness"

When we hunger and thirst for righteousness, we long for the completion of Jesus' saving work. He came into the world precisely to fulfill all righteousness, first in his own person and then to form it in us. When Jesus came to the Jordan to be baptized, he knew that his mission was to establish righteousness. When he asked to be baptized, John tried to prevent him, saying, "I need to be baptized by you, and do you come to me?" But Jesus answered him, "Let it be so now, for it is proper for us in this way to fulfill all righteousness" (Mt 3:14–15). In saying this, Jesus means first of all that he obeys the saving will of God, and that through his obedience he will fulfill God's plan in us.

In submitting to John's baptism, Jesus expresses his obedience to God's whole plan of salvation; he accepts the role of the suffering Servant. His baptism in water symbolizes his future baptism in blood on the cross. As Jesus comes out of the water, the Spirit of God descends upon him like a dove (cf. Mt 3:16). This symbolizes how, through his sacrificial sufferings and glorification, Jesus will communicate the Holy Spirit to all of us.

The Father responds to Jesus' obedient acceptance of this mission by declaring: "This is my Son, the Beloved, with whom I am well pleased" (Mt 3:17). Thus he clearly indicates that Jesus is the servant of whom he had said through Isaiah: "Here is my servant, whom I uphold, my chosen, in whom my soul delights; I have put my spirit upon him; he will bring forth justice to the nations" (Is 42:1). Thus the Father introduces Jesus as the Righteous One who fulfills all righteousness, and brings this righteousness to the nations. Jesus accepts his mission to carry out God's will to save the world, the work of restoring creatures to righteousness.

Hunger and thirst for righteousness makes us ardently desire and seek the completion of God's saving work, not just in ourselves, but in all his people, and indeed in all humanity. This hunger and thirst spurs us to get involved in the messiah's mission of righteousness. It kindles a missionary spirit to extend the kingdom of righteousness.

Jesus expects this of us. He did not say to John the Baptist, "It is proper for *me* to fulfill all righteousness," but "It is proper for *us* to fulfill all righteousness" (Mt 3:15). Jesus wants all of us to get involved in completing his saving work.

This zeal manifests itself in various ways, according to each one's specific vocation. It can express itself in working for social justice, by bringing Christ's merciful love and care to the poor, oppressed, sick and homeless. Thus it reveals to God's suffering people his love and compassion. It can express itself by preaching and teaching the principles of righteousness, proclaiming the "Gospel of Life" and the "Splendor of Truth," as Pope John Paul II did in his encyclicals under those titles. It can express itself in our zeal for holiness in our daily lives, especially in our loving relationships with all God's people.

Our involvement in our Lord's mission sometimes requires of us a righteous anger at the injustices all around us, especially unjust economic and social structures that oppress the poor. This includes that outrageous violence done to the helpless innocent, the unborn who are aborted. A true Christian does not timidly accept injustice. Rather, in zeal for the holiness of God, he or she knows how to use rightly the God-given power of just anger. Only a false humility would refuse to get involved in establishing social justice.

To the extent that we as a people live in God's just order, with the help of his grace conforming our lives to his saving will, we already live in the kingdom. For the kingdom exists where righteousness exists, *the* righteousness, that overflows into mercy and compassion toward the poor and needy. To the extent that we help establish the kingdom, God satisfies our hunger and thirst for righteousness.

Righteousness and the Gift of Piety

Righteousness has two dimensions, the vertical and the horizontal: to be right with God and right with neighbor. Through the gift of piety, the Holy Spirit brings both these dimensions to perfection.

What is the Spirit's gift of piety? Isaiah lists the gifts of the Holy Spirit that will rest upon the messiah: "The Spirit of the Lord shall rest on him, the spirit of wisdom and understanding, the spirit of counsel and might, the spirit of knowledge and the fear of the Lord. His delight shall be in the fear of the Lord" (Is 11:2–3).

We do not find piety in this list, while it twice mentions fear of the Lord. But when the Bible was translated from Hebrew into Greek in the days before Jesus Christ, the translators rendered the first occurrence of "fear of the Lord" as "piety." When St. Jerome later translated the Bible into Latin, he too rendered it as *pietas*. That is why the Fathers of the Church comment on seven gifts of the Holy Spirit, including piety.

Was it good to translate "fear of the Lord" as "piety"? No doubt by the time the Hebrew Bible came to be translated into Greek, God's people, meditating on the text of Isaiah, had come to realize that fear of the Lord, a profound reverence for the majesty of God, also has its tender filial aspect. The people gradually came to reverence Yahweh, the mighty God of power, as Father. For example, in Trito-Isaiah we read, "You, O Lord, are our father; our Redeemer from of old is your name" (Is 63:16).

This word "redeemer" *(go'el)* originally meant "next of kin." In Israel's early family culture, the next of kin had the responsibility of redeeming his kin who were facing difficulties. When Yahweh made his covenant with Israel and adopted family terminology to express his covenant relationship with them, he came to be called "Redeemer, next of kin." This logically developed from using the word *ḥesed*, family loyalty, to describe God's covenant relationship with his people.

Similarly, the Latin word *pietas* signifies family loyalty and devotion, tender reverence for parents, and loving affection for brothers and sisters. Hence the word aptly describes our tender filial relationship with God our Father, and consequently our brotherly and sisterly affection for God's children. Just as being right with one's parents requires being right with one's sisters and brothers, so too in

God's family, to be right with God, we must be right with one another.

The Holy Spirit's gift of piety forms in us and brings to perfection these two dimensions of righteousness within the family of God. The Spirit in our hearts helps us cry, "Abba! Father!" But the cry "Father" does not ring true unless, inspired by the same Holy Spirit, we cry sincerely, "Brother! Sister!" That cry must sound forth not just in word, but in deeds: "Little children, let us love, not in word or speech, but in truth and action" (1 Jn 3:18). The Holy Spirit of piety impels us to reach out in mercy to all the sons and daughters of God our Father, the brothers and sisters for whom Christ died: "Whatever you did for one of these least brothers of mine, you did for me" (Mt 25:40 NAB). God requires of us this overflowing righteousness for admission into the kingdom.

St. Paul calls the Holy Spirit "the Spirit of his Son" (Gal 4:6). By the grace of justification, the Spirit of the Son sets us right with the Father in the filial obedience of Jesus his Son. As the initial grace of justification produces its full fruits in us, the Spirit of piety forms in our hearts the Son's tender compassion for everyone, and thus sets us right with neighbor.

Justification an Initial Grace

Justification by faith is an initial grace. It needs to grow and expand in two ways. First, justification establishes us in right relationship with God, "this grace in which we stand" (Rm 5:2). This relationship with God our Father grows in ever greater tenderness and intimacy through the Spirit's gift of piety: "God's love has been poured into our hearts through the Holy Spirit that has been given to us" (Rm 5:5). Our loving filial relationship with God can grow without limit. This is the vertical dimension of our righteousness.

Righteousness also expands into the horizontal dimension of rightness with all the brothers and sisters for whom Christ died (cf. 1 Cor 8:11). The initial grace of justification must bear this further fruit.

St. Paul calls this fruit "the harvest of righteousness," describing it in relation to the Spirit: "The fruit of the Spirit is love, joy, peace, patience, kindness, generosity, faithfulness, gentleness and self-control" (Gal 5:22).

Obviously these fruits flow from loving others. Why are they called fruits? As the mature product of a plant, fruit has a certain sweetness, satisfies hunger and gives enjoyment, like eating a cold juicy watermelon on a hot summer day. Only the fruits of righteousness, ripened in us by the Holy Spirit's gift of piety, satisfy our hunger and thirst for righteousness.

Love Requires Justice

St. Thomas Aquinas shows how the Holy Spirit's gift of piety forms in us two beatitudes, "Blessed are those who hunger and thirst for justice" and "Blessed are the merciful." Our filial relationship with God our Father and our fraternal relationship with one another require justice and mercy. Love cannot exist without justice. The overflowing righteousness Jesus invites us to calls for both justice and mercy.

Thomas shows how piety, reverence for God our Father, makes us ready and eager to act justly toward one another. We pay our debts and willingly give others their due, out of reverence for the Father of all and love for our brothers and sisters. Similarly, in giving to others over and above what strict justice requires, piety impels us to the fullness of generous mercy.

Thus piety, filial reverence for God, inspires both mercy and justice. It is a mercy to God to treat his children with justice. For love by its very nature deeply cares about the well-being of the loved ones. It does justice, giving to each person his or her rights.

Respect Is the Basic Act of Justice

The most fundamental act of justice in human relationships is respect for each person's human dignity. In describing brotherly and sisterly love, St. Paul puts respect first: "Love one another with mutual affection; outdo one another in showing honor" (Rm 12:10). Every human person deserves honor, because of their dignity as the brothers and sisters for whom Christ died. Each one is a son or daughter of God. Reverencing God as Father of all means respecting all his children.

Because respect is the most basic act of justice, all other acts of justice and mercy flow from it. The Holy Spirit's gift of piety makes it grow in us, leading us to reverence God our Father and all his children without exception.

Each one's personal autonomy deserves respect. Each one must be allowed to be the person God created them to be. For example, parents should allow their children to grow in keeping with their God-given endowments. All this is basic justice, part of the righteousness the true Christian hungers and thirsts for. True community will grow in the measure that all persons are treated in keeping with their human dignity. Given the freedom and opportunity to fully use their gifts and talents, they will be their true selves.

Though our Christian communities often fall short, as individuals our hunger and thirst for righteousness is satisfied to the degree we enjoy a deep personal integrity. Being right with God in increasing purity of heart, as peacemakers we can work for community as best we can, following St. Paul's directive, "So far as it depends on you, live peaceably with all" (Rm 12:18).

We can live this beatitude by bearing wrongs patiently and not taking offense, bearing grudges, nourishing resentment nor seeking vengeance. The God of righteousness will infallibly establish his kingdom where righteousness reigns. "In accordance with his promise, we wait for new

heavens and a new earth, where righteousness is at home"
(2 Pet 3:13).

The fourth beatitude contains all the others. We are
justified by faith only when in poverty of spirit, knowing
our sinfulness, "not seeking to establish our own righteousness, we have submitted to God's righteousness" in faith
(cf. Rm 10:3). We mourn over the lack of righteousness in
ourselves and in our communities. In meekness, we do not
nourish resentment, which can destroy community. To the
best of our ability we strive to live at peace with all. These
few examples show once again how all the beatitudes
interlink. Blessed are those who hunger and thirst for righteousness, for they shall be filled with "righteousness and
peace and joy in the Holy Spirit" (Rm 14:17).

15

The Merciful

Blessed are the merciful,
for they will receive mercy (Mt 5:7).

What is mercy? On two different occasions, Jesus quoted the prophet Hosea, "I desire mercy, not sacrifice" (Mt 9:13; 12:7). When Jesus was dining in the home of Matthew, his new disciple, some people complained that Jesus associated with tax collectors and sinners. He said, "Go and learn what this means, 'I desire mercy, not sacrifice'" (Mt 9:13).

We can go to the prophet Hosea to learn his meaning. Various English translations of Hosea 6:6 render the word "mercy" *(ḥesed)* differently: "mercy" (KJV), "love" (NAB), "loving-kindness" (MLV), "loyalty" (NEB), "steadfast love" (RSV), "piety" (GOODSPEED), "faithful love" (NJB), "a tender heart" (KNOX)—eight different versions of the Hebrew word Hosea used.

Ḥesed is translated so differently because no English word captures its richness. Jesus used the Aramaic equivalent of *ḥesed* when he said "Blessed are the merciful, for they will receive mercy." Perhaps "covenant love" best translates *ḥesed*. It is the love binding together the people of God in the covenant God made with them.

As we saw earlier, for the ancient Hebrews *ḥesed* meant family love and loyalty, concern and care for one another within the family. The family members showed mercy to one another. *Ḥesed* was help given in every situation, compassion and mercy even for wayward family members. *Ḥesed* was the virtue of family solidarity.

When God made his covenant with his people Israel, he accepted them as his family, and so the family word *ḥesed* was used to describe the covenant relationship. Repeatedly in the Scriptures God describes this relationship with his people as *ḥesed we 'emet*, "steadfast love and faithfulness." "The Lord, the Lord, a God merciful and gracious, slow to anger, and abounding in *steadfast love and faithfulness*" (Ex 34:6). The words occur at least thirty times in the psalms.

Just as God shows *ḥesed* or covenant love toward his people, they are to show it to one another in all their relationships. The prophet Hosea called them to do this and to repent of their failures.

Like Hosea, Jesus emphasized Israel's call to covenant fidelity: "Do not think that I have come to abolish the law or the prophets; I have come not to abolish but to fulfill" (Mt 5:17). God's people fulfill the Law when they live the overflowing righteousness that flows from *ḥesed*, covenant love, mercy.

Ḥesed and righteousness are the same thing seen from two different points of view. Righteousness sees it from the perspective of justice, while *ḥesed* sees justice as the fundamental expression of covenant love. True love requires justice. Love always does what is right.

Ḥesed, loyal and merciful family love, unites God with his people, and the people with God and with one another. *Ḥesed*, mutual family support, is the community virtue making us the one family of God. *Ḥesed* leads to the peacemaking that shows we are children of God.

While we tend to think of mercy only as compassion for sinners, it goes far beyond that. It includes everything God's people do to support one another. But since the temptation often arises to reject and despise sinful members, Jesus emphasizes that covenant love reaches out even to them: "Take care that you do not despise one of these little ones" who go astray (Mt 18:10). Seek them out and mercifully receive them back, as the shepherd leaves the ninety-nine sheep and seeks the one that has strayed.

Hesed or mercy is essentially a family or community virtue. St. Paul stresses this when he writes, "Be kind to one another, tenderhearted, forgiving one another, as God in Christ has forgiven you" (Eph 4:32).

Do not all of us tend to go astray, and so need compassion from our sisters and brothers in the Lord? The Mass begins with a penitential rite, in which we seek reconciliation with one another and with God. In our Christian life, as covenant love, we daily exercise mercy toward one another.

This loyal, steadfast covenant love, this mercy and compassion for one another, is the mercy God prefers over sacrifice. When Hosea presents God as saying, "I desire steadfast love and not sacrifice" (Hos 6:6), he is asking, "What good would sacrifices and holocausts be without covenant love and compassion?" We turn the Eucharistic liturgy into a lie if we come to it with disunity, lacking love and forgiveness.

The Universality of Mercy

The other context in which Jesus quotes Hosea's words confirms the wisdom of interpreting "mercy" in the broad sense of *hesed*. On a Sabbath, the disciples were passing through the grain fields. Feeling hungry, they began to pluck and eat heads of grain. When a few Pharisees said that they were violating the Sabbath law, Jesus corrected their interpretation of the law. He called attention to the covenant love that is the true intent of the law, a love that should be delighted that the poor disciples' needs were being met. Fidelity to the Law of Moses is a matter of loving relationships with all of God's people in covenant fidelity.

Each time Jesus uses the word "mercy" in Matthew's Gospel, it has the full meaning of *hesed*. For example, when two blind men approached him and cried out, "Have mercy on us, Son of David," they were asking him to show them covenant love by responding to their need. All true works of mercy spring from covenant love. Mercy must penetrate our whole life within the new and eternal covenant, a covenant love that permeates all our daily relationships. Since no one is sufficient unto self, but all of us are poor and needy, we all need mercy. Mercy sustains our daily life as people of God.

This context of *hesed* as fidelity to the law of Moses illuminates Jesus' answer to the question, "'Teacher, which commandment in the law is the greatest?' He said to him, '"You shall love the Lord your God with all your heart, and with all your soul, and with all your mind." This is the greatest and first commandment. And a second is like it: "You shall love your neighbor as yourself." On these two commandments hang all the law and the prophets'" (Mt 22:36–40). Is not this Jesus' way of saying that fidelity to the law is *hesed*, covenant love? All the commandments give directions for loving.

Love of neighbor always involves compassion or mercy, for who has no faults? All the virtues St. Paul lists for dealing with people presume that others are far from perfect, so we all need patience and compassion: "As God's chosen ones, holy and beloved, clothe yourselves with compassion, kindness, humility, meekness, and patience. Bear with one another and, if anyone has a complaint against another, forgive each other; just as the Lord has forgiven you, so you also must forgive" (Col 3:12–13).

No wonder, then, that the word *ḥesed* is translated "mercy," for our love for one another involves compassion for human frailty. From the earliest days of Hebrew usage, *ḥesed* meant to respond to human neediness—from an infant crying for food to an elderly person on a deathbed. By nature we are family, and need one another. Family love, the original meaning of *ḥesed*, supports the weakness of the family members. This is true of the whole family of God, both in the covenant of Israel, and in the new and eternal covenant in the blood of Christ.

All the beatitudes are community virtues, and each beatitude reflects one of the many facets of *ḥesed*, covenant love. As an all-pervading quality, *ḥesed* flows into every aspect of our daily life together, just as blood flows through our body, nourishing every cell. We benefit fully from covenant love only when we exercise it.

Jesus offered the supreme act of covenant love by his sacrifice on the cross, showing mercy to us all, and making with us the new and eternal covenant in his blood. By his sacrifice, communicated to us especially in the Eucharist, Jesus empowers us to love one another as he loves us, and thus fulfill the wish of God who says, "I desire mercy, not sacrifice."

"Blessed are the merciful"—those who live the fullness of covenant love in their daily life—"for they shall receive mercy." The need for compassion and forgiveness is our greatest need.

"Doing" Covenant Love

Ḥesed or mercy is not simply an emotional feeling of pity or compassion. The Hebrew Scriptures never speak of "feeling *ḥesed*." They speak only of "doing *ḥesed*." *Ḥesed* is something we do, not just something we feel. It is not enough to feel compassion; we must act on that compassion. Thus it is possible lovingly to forgive someone who has offended us without feeling any special warmth of affection for the person. Merciful forgiveness is primarily an act of love, an act of the will.

Similarly the obligation of doing *ḥesed* in everyday life does not require feeling enthusiastic about it. How many parents feel enthusiastic about getting up in the middle of the night to change a crying baby's diaper? We may not feel like doing something, yet we can will to do it with love. Enthusiasm certainly helps. But acting even when one does not feel like it may show a deeper, truer love than a passing emotional warmth would.

We "do" *ḥesed* when we do the works of merciful love. *Ḥesed* feeds the hungry, shelters the homeless, clothes the naked, visits the sick, helps the sinner and the wavering, counsels the ignorant and the doubtful. *Ḥesed* includes all the actions of covenant love, including such mundane deeds as scrubbing a dirty child in the bathtub, or teaching him or her the basic ways of morality. *Ḥesed* also includes patriotism, deeds of loyalty within the family of our nation.

A striking example in the Letter of James clearly shows that mercy is something we *do:* "If a brother or sister is naked and lacks daily food, and one of you says to them, 'Go in peace; keep warm and eat your fill,' and yet you do not supply their bodily needs, what is the good of that? So faith by itself, if it has no works, is dead" (Jas 2:15–17).

Jesus Does Mercy

Jesus performed many works of mercy, curing the sick and expelling demons. Matthew says:

> This was to fulfill what had been spoken through
> the prophet Isaiah:

"Here is my servant, whom I have chosen,
   my beloved, with whom my soul is well pleased.
I will put my Spirit upon him,
   and he will proclaim justice to the Gentiles.
He will not wrangle or cry aloud,
   nor will anyone hear his voice in the streets.
He will not break a bruised reed
   or quench a smoldering wick
until he brings justice to victory.
   And in his name the Gentiles will hope"
     (Mt 12:17–21).

"He will not wrangle or cry out." The meek and humble Jesus will not argue and fight with his critics. He ignores them and continues to do mercy.

"He will not break a bruised reed." He will not crush the poor and needy. He will not reproach them, blaming them for their misery, as we so often do, but he will lift them up, healing their ills.

"He will not quench a smoldering wick," but will re-kindle in sinners the flame of divine love.

By his works of mercy, "he brings justice to victory." That is, he establishes the overflowing righteousness of the kingdom. He sets all things right by his deeds of mercy; he establishes merciful love as the law of his kingdom.

Despite opposition, Jesus quietly continues his works of mercy, and eventually suffers and dies on the cross doing mercy, giving his life in ransom for the many (cf. Mt 20:28).

He shows compassion even to his persecutors. As they nail him to the cross, he prays for all who are responsible for his death (and that includes us): "Father, forgive them; for they do not know what they are doing" (Lk 23:34). Thus he shows supreme mercy, the forgiveness of sins.

This background helps us understand what he means when he says, "Blessed are the merciful, for they will receive mercy" (Mt 5:7). We are all to join him in his mission of mercy. Mercy, *hesed,* the lifeblood of Christian life, is the blood of Jesus, shed for our sins, flowing through his body, the Church.

In offering himself in sacrifice for the forgiveness of sinners he shows supreme mercy. He does what he asked us to do in the Sermon on the Mount, saying, "Love your enemies and pray for those who persecute you, so that you may be children of your Father in heaven" (Mt 5:44–45). With Jesus, we not only suffer persecution for righteousness' sake, but we suffer with Jesus for our persecutors, asking the Father to forgive them. Thus the supreme mercy of the cross continues among us.

"Be merciful, just as your Father is merciful" (Lk 6:36). The merciful Father cares about the sinner as well as the innocent: "He makes his sun rise on the evil and on the good, and sends rain on the righteous and on the unrighteous" (Mt 5:45). In our loving mercy toward all, friend or foe, we are truly children of the Father. As peacemakers we grant forgiveness readily.

Mercy: A Community Quality

Together as a people, we experience the universal poverty and misery of sinful humanity, and the need of all for God's saving grace. Together we respond to one another's poverty. Our merciful covenant love shows itself in the generous help we extend to one another in every area of life, and in the ready forgiveness we grant to one another, just as God, in Christ, has forgiven us.

Together, each day we pray, "Our Father...forgive us our trespasses, as we forgive those who trespass against us."

All this is what Jesus means when he says, "Blessed are the merciful, for they will receive mercy." Mutual loving help marks this happy community. "Everything they owned was held in common.... There was not a needy person among them" (Acts 4:32, 34). For in God's family, in love's readiness, each one considers his or her own material and spiritual gifts at the service of those in need. Mercy, *ḥesed*, is truly the life-blood of the People of God.

16

The Pure of Heart

Blessed are the pure in heart,
for they will see God (Mt 5:8).

The eight beatitudes depict the full joy of being with God, seeing him face to face, at home in his love with all his children, at peace with everyone. This happiness comes only to the pure of heart.

"The pure of heart shall see God" sums up some verses of Psalm 24. This psalm lays down the conditions for living in God's presence and enjoying intimate communion with him:

> Who shall ascend the hill of the Lord?
>   And who shall stand in his holy place?
> Those who have clean hands and pure hearts,
>   who do not lift up their souls to what is false,
>   and do not swear deceitfully.
> They will receive blessing from the Lord,
>   and vindication from the God of their salvation.
> Such is the company of those who seek him,
>   who seek the face of the God of Jacob (Ps 24:3–6).

Psalm 24 is our best commentary on this beatitude. The psalm speaks of clean hands as well as pure hearts. "Clean hands" stands for righteous external actions, while "pure hearts" indicates the interior source of these actions. Purity of moral action presupposes purity of heart.

Our Lord makes this point again and again in the Sermon on the Mount. It is not enough to avoid sinful actions such as adultery. One must keep the heart pure. "I say to you that everyone who looks at a woman with lust has already committed adultery with her in his heart" (Mt 5:28). Again, it is not enough to avoid murder; one must not nourish anger in the heart (cf. Mt 5:21–22). Jesus taught a spirituality of the heart, the wellspring of our actions.

In biblical language, the heart is the source of thought and will, and therefore of action. Our thoughts, intentions, plans and actions proceed from the heart, which must be kept pure. "Keep your heart with all vigilance, for from it flow the springs of life" (Prov 4:23).

Moreover, the purity of heart necessary for seeing God and living in his presence goes far beyond moral purity, or purity in thought and action. It is first of all sincerity toward God, single-heartedness in seeking him. A pure moral life flows only from a heart pure and sincere toward God.

Psalm 24 speaks of this single-heartedness toward God. "Who can stand in his holy place? The clean of hand and pure of heart, who are not devoted to idols, who have not sworn falsely" (Ps 24:3–4 NAB).

"Who are not devoted to idols" has also been translated "whose heart is not set on vanities" (NJB). Scripture often refers to idols as "vanities."

The pure of heart are "not devoted to idols." They do not divide their heart among many gods, but focus it entirely on the Lord, the one true God. Wholehearted toward him, they show single-hearted love and devotion to him. Hebrew has a word for it: *tamim,* wholehearted, sincere. Utterly sincere toward God and neighbor, they "do not swear deceitfully" (Ps 24:4). So this beatitude is sometimes translated, "Blessed are the single-hearted, for they shall see God."

Psalm 27 also speaks of this single-heartedness. "One thing I asked of the Lord, that will I seek after: to live in the house of the Lord all the days of my life, to behold the beauty of the Lord, and to inquire in his temple" (Ps 27:4).

Purity of heart goes beyond the moral purity that consists in practicing the moral virtues, such as chastity, temperance, justice. Purity of heart concerns our direct relationship with God in faith, hope and love, the three theological virtues. We might call it theological purity, purity in our relationship with God, being utterly sincere with him, single-hearted in seeking him alone.

In the Sermon on the Mount, Jesus warns us against idolizing earthly riches. "Do not store up for yourselves treasures on earth, where moth and rust consume and where thieves break in and steal: but store up for yourselves treasures in heaven, where neither moth nor rust consumes and where thieves do not break in and steal. For where your treasure is, there your heart will be also" (Mt 6:19–21). Clearly, purity of heart is not only freedom from lust, but from greed, ambition and the like.

Moral purity of heart and action flows from theological purity of heart, focusing the heart on God alone in faith, hope and love. The more firmly that faith, hope and love attach our hearts to God, the more thoroughly will they be detached from all that would draw us away from God. The Holy Spirit dwelling in our hearts and filling us with love of God forms this moral purity in us: "If by the Spirit you put to death the deeds of the body, you will live" (Rm 8:13).

Pure hearts desire to live in the house of the Lord, at home with the Father and at peace with all his children. Clinging to God as their only treasure, desires for things apart from God do not easily agitate them. A lack of possessions does not easily disturb them. They have the fortitude even to face persecution.

The beatitudes of righteousness and mercy also contribute to their purity of heart. Being just and merciful to others requires dying to selfishness. God purifies our hearts of selfishness when, for love of him, we reach out to others in mercy, and live with them in peace and justice.

Psalm 15 speaks of seeing God and living in his presence, emphasizing the moral virtues relating to neighbor:

> O Lord, who may abide in your tent?
>   Who may dwell on your holy hill?
> Those who walk blamelessly, and do what is right,
>   and speak the truth from their heart;
> who do not slander with their tongue,
>   and do no evil to their friends,
>   nor take up a reproach against their neighbors;
> in whose eyes the wicked are despised,
>   but who honor those who fear the Lord;
> who stand by their oath even to their hurt;
> who do not lend money at interest,
>   and do not take a bribe against the innocent.
> Those who do these things shall never be moved
>   (Ps 15).

In short, we need to deal uprightly with our neighbor if we wish to dwell with God on his holy mountain. Seeing God requires both moral and theological purity. "For the Lord is righteous; he loves righteous deeds; the upright shall behold his face" (Ps 11:7).

"The peace of God which surpasses all understanding" (Phil 4:7) fills the pure of heart, making them peacemakers. Their peaceful, serene hearts easily mirror the beauty of God, whose presence they enjoy.

Does this mean that acquiring purity of heart will enable us to enjoy God's presence incessantly? No, for no matter what degree of purity of heart we have attained, no matter how lively our faith, hope and love, no matter how perfect our humility and meekness, our mercy and compassion, we will not automatically enjoy the presence of God. For we cannot control how God will manifest himself to us.

Purity of heart prepares us to receive God's self-manifestation when he wills to give it. Purity of heart removes the obstacles to his self-giving, but of itself does not win it. God pours out his contemplative graces only as pure gift, and we cannot earn them or force them by our purity of heart. We can only prepare our hearts to receive these graces and then await his good pleasure, for he gives them only as he sees fit. When he hides his presence from the pure of heart, they can only wait for him with ardent longing. "I sought him, but did not find him; I called him, but he gave no answer" (Song 5:6).

Once the pure of heart have tasted the goodness of the Lord, they ardently desire to taste him still more. When he hides his presence, they ravenously desire that he manifest himself again. But when he delays doing this, they can only wait for him in patience. Only in heaven will God completely satisfy their desire to see him. In this life they will experience a certain amount of discontent, an ardent longing for the Lord's presence. This discontent is all the greater the more deeply they have tasted of his goodness. As long as we remain on earth, we must continue to seek the Lord.

Single-heartedness in seeking the Lord involves purity of intention. In the Sermon on the Mount, Jesus teaches the need for purity of intention in all our good works. "Take care not to perform righteous deeds in order that people may see them; otherwise you will have no recompense from your heavenly Father" (Mt 6:1 NAB). Jesus tells us to seek God alone in all we do, doing it out of pure love of God, not to be seen by others.

"Those who have clean hands and pure hearts...will

receive blessing from the Lord.... Such is the company of those who seek him, who seek the face of the God of Jacob" (Ps 24:4–6). The expression "seek the face of God" frequently occurs in the Bible. "My soul thirsts for God, for the living God. When shall I come and behold the face of God?" (Ps 42:2). The word "face" expresses the truth that God is a living person, who desires "face to face" communion with us. To seek God's face means to seek his personal presence, to win his good will and kindness, to obtain his blessings. "O God, you are my God, I seek you, my soul thirsts for you" (Ps 63:1). "The upright shall behold his face" (Ps 11:7).

To seek the face of God is to seek personal communion with him, to be face to face with him on good terms. In the official blessing in Israel's liturgy, the priest would say, "The Lord make his face to shine upon you, and be gracious to you" (Nm 6:25). That is, may he smile upon you and receive you favorably.

The pure of heart enjoy this smile. They see God and rest in his presence. Even when he seems to hide himself, at least they experience the peace that flows from purity of conscience.

Whoever loves God and seeks his face, thirsting for him in ardent desire and hope, often has to wait patiently for God to reveal himself: "My soul thirsts for God, for the living God. When shall I come and behold the face of God? My tears have been my food day and night, while people say to me continually, 'Where is your God?'... Why are you cast down, O my soul, and why are you disquieted within me? Hope in God; for I shall again praise him, my help and my God" (Ps 42:2–6).

How often we must wait for God to manifest his presence! He delays revealing himself so that our longing and desire for him might grow. Desire broadens our heart to receive him. Waiting for him with loving desire purifies our heart still more.

The pure of heart shall see God face to face in his glory. But even now on earth, they often "taste and see that the Lord is good" (Ps 34:8) as he manifests his presence in contemplative graces, and in various other blessings that show his loving care.

The pure of heart are the poor in spirit, the humble of heart purified of arrogance and pride. They are the meek, purified of anger, resentment, aggressiveness, violence and vengeance. With gentleness they respond kindly toward others. They are the sorrowful whose hearts have been purified by contrition for sin. Their hunger and thirst for righteousness has purified their hearts of all injustice. They are the merciful, who, purified of self-centeredness, have rushed to help others in their neediness. They are peace-makers, for their hearts do not cling to the things over which other people may battle. A person who possesses any one of the beatitudes possesses them all.

Those who possess the beatitudes are "the little ones" of the first beatitude, to whom God reveals the mysteries of the kingdom. "I thank you, Father, Lord of heaven and earth, because you have hidden these things from the wise and the intelligent and have revealed them to infants.... No one knows the Son except the Father, and no one knows the Father except the Son and anyone to whom the Son chooses to reveal him" (Mt 11:25, 27). Blessed are the pure of heart, for they will see God.

17

The Peacemakers

Blessed are the peacemakers,
for they will be called children of God (Mt 5:9).

Throughout Matthew's Gospel, Jesus refers to God as "your Father." By calling God "your Father," he also teaches us what it means to be God's children. As sons and daughters of God, peacemakers are like their heavenly Father. Their peacemaking shows God's life in them. For example, peacemaking calls for forgiving enemies, a sure sign of a child of God. "Love your enemies, and pray for those who persecute you, so that you may be children of your Father in heaven" (Mt 5:44–45).

Just as peacemaking belongs to God's own deepest nature, God's children possess this quality too. Scripture often calls God "the God of peace" (Rm 15:33; 16:20; Heb 13:20) to indicate that peacemaking is of his very essence, inseparable from his nature, and the source of peace in his people. So too peacemaking marks God's children, as it marked the life of Jesus.

Matthew presents Jesus as a peacemaker. On Palm Sunday, he rides into Jerusalem on a donkey, bringing peace:

"Tell the daughter of Zion, look, your king is coming to you, humble, and mounted on a donkey, and on a colt, the foal of a donkey" (Mt 21:5). In quoting that one line, Matthew wants us to recall the whole passage of Zechariah:

> Lo, your king comes to you...humble and riding on a donkey, on a colt, the foal of a donkey.... He will cut off the chariot from Ephraim and the war-horse from Jerusalem; and the battle bow shall be cut off, and he shall command peace to the nations (Zech 9:9–10).

Jesus comes to banish war. "For all the boots of the tramping warriors and all the garments rolled in blood shall be burned as fuel for the fire" (Is 9:5). Jesus does not come on a fiery warhorse, but on a lowly donkey, to signify he brings peace. He does not come to win a kingdom by violence. He comes to reconcile and bring peace to Israel and to all the nations.

In citing various scriptural texts in his Gospel, Matthew associates them with Jesus as a peacemaker. Thus, when the Magi come to Jerusalem seeking the newborn king of the Jews, the chief priests and scribes quote to them the prophet Micah: "And you, Bethlehem, in the land of Judah, are by no means least among the rulers of Judah; for from you shall come a ruler who is to shepherd my people Israel" (Mt 2:6; Micah 5:1–4). In Micah the text continues, "He himself will be peace" (5:4 NJB).

When Jesus enters the city, meek and riding on an ass, the people acclaim him, saying, "Blessed is the one who comes in the name of the Lord!" (Mt 21:9). Jesus comes with the authority of the God of peace, with the mission to carry out God's work of peace. Like his Father in heaven, the Son brings peace, and he teaches his disciples to make peace. Speaking of "your Father in heaven," he says, "You are the light of the world.... Let your light shine before others, so that they may see your good works and give glory to your Father in heaven" (Mt 5:14, 16). Their good deeds show that Jesus' disciples are like their heavenly Father, and so are rightly called his children. These good deeds are works of love, works seeking reconciliation and peace.

In speaking against anger, for example, Jesus says, "When you are offering your gift at the altar, if you remember that your brother or sister has something against you, leave your gift there before the altar and go; first be reconciled to your brother or sister, and then come and offer your gift" (Mt 5:23–24).

Similarly, in speaking against divorce, Jesus expects husband and wife to make peace with each other, for he forbids divorce (cf. Mt 5:31–32). Fidelity in marriage among the children of God reveals that God's mature children know how to make peace.

Peacemaking also includes love of enemies, and shows in God's children the perfection of their heavenly Father. Jesus requires that we love all, not just those who love us. After teaching us in the Lord's Prayer to call God Father, Jesus comments on this prayer, saying, "If you forgive others their trespasses, your heavenly Father will also forgive you; but if you do not forgive others, neither will your Father forgive your trespasses" (Mt 6:14–15). Peacemaking requires daily forgiveness. We receive God's forgiveness and live at peace with him because we forgive and live at peace with one another.

Peacemaking operates not only in moments of stress when we offend one another and seek reconciliation, but in all the activities of God's children. All our positive works of love, deeds of mercy and acts of rejoicing in one another promote peace.

Each of the eight beatitudes fosters peace. Jesus calls the poor in spirit "the little ones," who in humility have become like little children. Their humility has purified them of the pride and arrogance that destroy peace.

Peace also requires meekness. If poverty of spirit makes us little before God, meekness makes us gentle toward others. It excludes anger, irritability, bitterness and ill-humor. Meekness fosters mildness, kindness and gentleness. As the family of God, the meek possess the land in harmony and peace, enjoying God's blessings together. The meek practice peacefulness with serenity and mercy, always ready to make allowances for others.

In a special way, those who hunger and thirst for righteousness promote peace, for peace requires justice. It also calls for mutual trust.

The Hebrew word for peace, *shalom,* came to mean the sum of blessings brought by the messiah, "Prince of Peace" (Is 9:6). Justice and peace are so inseparable that they embrace: "Steadfast love and faithfulness will meet; righteousness and peace will kiss each other" (Ps 85:10). Righteousness, being right with God and also with one another and all of creation, establishes peace and harmony. All this is the work of the messiah.

He will set us right with God: "They will not hurt or destroy on all my holy mountain; for the earth will be full of the knowledge of the Lord as the waters cover the sea" (Is 11:9). In biblical language, knowledge of the Lord means love of God expressed in fidelity to his will. This fidelity establishes righteousness and will bring about peace.

The messiah will also set us right with one another: "Ephraim shall not be jealous of Judah, and Judah shall not be hostile toward Ephraim" (Is 11:13). He will set us right with all creation: "The wolf shall live with the lamb...the calf and the lion and the fatling together, and a little child shall lead them" (Is 11:6).

Peacemaking begins with seeking forgiveness and reconciliation. From this beginning, the true peacemaker works in a positive way to establish justice in all human relationships. "A harvest of righteousness is sown in peace for those who make peace" (Jas 3:18). We work for peace, plant it and cultivate it, like a gardener tending exquisite roses, and it bears fruit in righteousness, another word for peace. Peace reigns when right order reigns in human life.

Moreover, the peacemaker practices all the works of mercy. "Blessed are the merciful, for they will receive mercy." The children of God show mercy just as the heavenly Father shows mercy. This mercy not only forgives others, but also provides for their needs. As children of the Father, we help saints and sinners alike in our works of mercy, and thus practice peace.

Peacemakers do not only reconcile enemies. First of all, peacemakers possess the deep interior personal peace that flows from purity of heart. In purity of heart, they see God, and that peace radiates to those around them.

In purity of heart, they treasure God above all else, so they have no desire to fight with others to get things. Because they trust completely in their heavenly Father, they can face troubles serenely. They believe Jesus' words, "Your Father knows what you need before you ask him" (Mt 6:8). "Strive first for the kingdom of God and his righteousness, and all these things will be given to you as well" (Mt 6:33). In purity of heart, seeking God alone, they possess "the peace of God, which surpasses all understanding" (Phil 4:7).

Those whom Jesus sends forth into the world proclaim peace wherever they go. "As you enter the house, greet it. If the house is worthy, let your peace come upon it; but if it is not worthy, let your peace return to you" (Mt 10:12–13).

A peacemaker lives all the beatitudes, including the eighth, "Blessed are those who are persecuted for righteousness' sake, for theirs is the kingdom of heaven" (Mt 5:10).

The peacemaker suffers persecution patiently in union with the Prince of Peace, who meek and riding upon an ass, brought peace to the world by suffering the rejection of the cross. "For in him all the fullness of God was pleased to dwell, and through him God was pleased to reconcile to himself all things, whether on earth or in heaven, by making peace through the blood of his cross" (Col 1:19–20). Those who suffer persecution with him, pray for their persecutors as he did, "Father, forgive them."

"Upon him was the punishment that made us whole" (Is 53:5). The word "whole" translates *shalom,* which also means peace. Peace is the wholeness we enjoy when we are right with God, with one another, and with all creation, in Christ Jesus our Lord. "For he is our peace.... In one body through the cross" he has reconciled to God all who were divided. "For through him, both of us have access in one Spirit to the Father" (Eph 2:14, 16, 18).

Peacemakers are sons and daughters of the God of peace. All eight beatitudes, working together as one, make us like our Father in heaven. Blessed be Jesus our Peace-maker, for in him we are all children of God!

18

The Persecuted

Blessed are those who are persecuted for righteousness' sake, for theirs is the kingdom of heaven (Mt 5:10).

The kingdom consists in righteousness, which contradicts those values and practices of society that are opposed to the Gospel. That is why those who live the beatitudes to a high degree will inevitably suffer persecution. Enduring that persecution is itself a supreme beatitude that crowns all the others. For persecution will not shake those who are solid and advanced in practicing all the beatitudes. They will persevere without denying our Lord.

The kingdom already belongs to those who endure severe persecution for Jesus. For the reign of God has already begun for those who practice all the beatitudes. Even now they can begin to enjoy the happiness of the kingdom.

Jesus speaks of this joy of the kingdom, enjoyed even in the midst of persecution, saying, "Blessed are you when people revile and persecute you and utter all kinds of evil against you falsely on my account. Rejoice and be glad, for your reward is great in heaven" (Mt 5:11–12).

We can rejoice even in the midst of persecution, crowned with the supreme beatitude that perfects all the others. We rejoice not because we suffer, but because we possess the righteousness that provokes the persecution.

One could object to this, saying, "No, you do not rejoice because of your righteousness, but because you love Christ for whose sake you suffer persecution. Joy flows from this love."

This is true, because wholehearted love of God brings the fullness of righteousness. To rejoice in righteousness is to rejoice in one's relationship with God in faith, hope and love, the basic elements of holiness. The joy of loving union with God flows from the joy of righteousness.

Jesus uses superlative terms when he speaks of the happiness this eighth beatitude brings. He does not only say, "Happy are those who suffer persecution." He says that those who suffer persecution rejoice exultantly and leap for joy: "Blessed are you when people hate you, and when they exclude you, revile you, and defame you on account of the Son of Man. Rejoice in that day and leap for joy, for surely your reward is great in heaven" (Lk 6:22–23).

St. Peter, too, gives an eloquent homily on the eighth beatitude:

> Rejoice insofar as you are sharing Christ's suffering, so that you may also be glad and shout for joy when his glory is revealed. If you are reviled for the name of Christ, you are blessed, because the spirit of glory, which is the Spirit of God, is resting on you (1 Pet 4:13–14).

The Holy Spirit, the Spirit of glory who rests on us, enables us to rejoice while suffering for Christ. The Spirit's presence forms in us love of Christ and of God, and strengthens us to practice all the beatitudes. We can rejoice in persecution because we experience the peace and joy that flow from love of God and all the other virtues. St. Paul says that the kingdom is "righteousness and peace and joy in the Holy Spirit" (Rm 14:17). As we grow in righteousness, we come more fully into God's reign, and experience more deeply the peace and joy resulting from it.

Thus the eighth beatitude crowns all the beatitudes. The poor in spirit humbly trust in the heavenly Father. The beatitude of meekness enables them to endure persecution patiently without anger or hatred. While mourning over opposition and affliction, joy in the Lord comforts them.

They can practice such patience and love because their hunger and thirst for righteousness has moved them to strive for it in every situation. Being right with God, within themselves and with others, they can forgive their persecutors. Their well-being in virtue brings peace and joy.

The beatitude of mercy impels them to show mercy and forgive even those who persecute them. "Love your enemies and pray for those who persecute you" (Mt 5:44). The supreme act of mercy is to ask God's mercy upon one's enemies, as Stephen prayed for those who were stoning him, saying, "Lord, do not hold this sin against them" (Acts 7:60).

In purity of heart, like Stephen, they see God (cf. Acts 7:55) and love him so intensely that they love even their enemies. They are like the Father who "makes his sun rise on the evil and on the good, and sends rain on the righteous and on the unrighteous" (Mt 5:45).

As children of God they make peace, offering themselves in sacrifice with Jesus for their persecutors. They make his prayer on the cross their own, "Father, forgive them; for they do not know what they are doing" (Lk 23:34).

Suffering persecution for righteousness' sake shows that they practice all the beatitudes, so that they can "rejoice... and leap for joy" (Lk 6:23). They rejoice because of their love for God and neighbor, this love that is humble and meek, righteous and merciful, pure in heart and peaceful toward others. The sense of well-being that comes with virtue brings deep spiritual joy.

In short, they possess all the theological and moral virtues, which open them to possessing God. With hearts purified by *faith,* they see God. In poverty of spirit, humbly knowing their littleness and neediness, they *hope* in God alone, whom they *love* above all things. *Meekness* tempers anger, and *patience* helps them deal with the evils of life.

In their hunger and thirst for righteousness, they practice the cardinal virtue of *justice,* that sets them right in relationships with others. As children in God's family, their love for the heavenly Father and for all his children moves them to make peace.

Prudence works in all the beatitudes, for prudence guides love. In every situation it points out the most loving thing to do.

The cardinal virtue of *fortitude* works powerfully in the eighth beatitude, strengthening the righteous to hold fast under persecution. The virtue of fortitude achieves its perfection only under the influence of the Holy Spirit's gift of fortitude. "If you are reviled for the name of Christ, you are blessed, because the spirit of glory, which is the Spirit of God, is resting on you" (1 Pet 4:14).

Martyrdom crowns and perfects Christian morality, the supreme expression of the eighth beatitude. In his encyclical *The Splendor of Truth,* Pope John Paul II teaches that martyrdom is "an affirmation of the inviolability of the moral order" (n. 92). The moral order God established is so sacred that a fervent Christian is ready to die rather than violate God's law. "There are truths and moral values for which one must be prepared to give up one's life" (n. 94).

One who gives up his or her life for the truth of God practices the eighth beatitude in the highest degree. Immediate entry into glory crowns the act of martyrdom. Those who are strong enough to suffer persecution for the truth firmly practice all the beatitudes, and have begun to enjoy the fruits of the kingdom of God.

19

"Seek Humility"

"Blessed are the poor in spirit, for theirs is the kingdom of heaven." This could also be said as, "Blessed are the humble of heart; the kingdom of heaven is theirs." Only the humble are fully open to receive God's richest blessings. "God opposes the proud, but gives grace to the humble" (1 Pet 5:5).

The prophet Zephaniah says, "Seek humility" (Zeph 2:3). The prophet urges us to cooperate with God's purpose of forming for himself a holy remnant, "a people humble and lowly" (Zeph 3:12). We need to actively seek humility, cultivating it in cooperation with God's purifying work. We choose to develop humility; it doesn't happen automatically. "Seek humility."

How do we seek it? Humility is truth. Humility recognizes and admits the truth about ourselves and the truth about God. Humility means realizing and honestly admitting our poverty and neediness. "God chose what is foolish in the world to shame the wise; God chose what is weak in the world to shame the strong; God chose what is low and despised in the world, things that are not, to reduce to nothing things that are" (1 Cor 1:27–28).

Usually we learn humility in the serious trials of life. We finally have the humility to admit we are poor and needy only if we have experienced suffering, loss, hunger, sickness, tears and sorrow. Then Jesus can say to us, "Blessed are you who are poor, for yours is the kingdom of God. Blessed are you who are hungry now, for you will be filled. Blessed are you who weep now, for you will laugh" (Lk 6:20–21). Just by being what they are, the humble and the suffering draw Jesus' blessing on them. God loves the poor and needy. They move Jesus to compassion, and he responds to them in mercy. To be needy and helpless opens our hearts to receive the blessings Jesus gives. Accepting this reality, we learn humility and trust in God, and thus become, by his grace, more fully sons and daughters of God.

To seek and find humility we must recognize and admit our deepest poverty, something far more radical than material poverty. We need to acknowledge our spiritual poverty—our ignorance of God, our limited understanding of his ways, our spiritual blindness, our lack of virtue, our weakness in doing good, our failure to grow in holiness, our laziness in making efforts to grow, our flawed love, love spoiled by selfishness.

In short, we need to recognize and admit everything in ourselves that spells sin. In sincere humility we must say, "God, be merciful to me, a sinner" (Lk 18:13).

The humility of the first beatitude, "Blessed are the poor in spirit," includes knowing that we are sinners. It includes mourning over our sin and seeking God's mercy. Our lack of holiness makes us hunger and thirst for it, as the gift of God's mercy. Each of the eight beatitudes in its own way expresses humility.

Blessed mourning over sin is not self-pity over the evil effects of our sins, or feeling sorry for ourselves because our sinful falls hurt our pride. The beatitude of mourning over sin centers our attention on God, not on ourselves. We repent that we have offended the Holy One, the God of love. True contrition expresses love's sorrow that we have offended God who loves us. Thus genuine contrition includes humility and love.

Do we collapse into discouragement or despair when we

recognize our profound spiritual poverty, our sinfulness, our deficiency in love and virtue? Not at all. We take refuge in the Lord.

In the humble person, two things always go together: knowing one's neediness, and hoping in the Lord, trusting fully in God. We trust in God because his merciful love reaches out to our humble neediness.

"Seek the Lord, all you humble of the land," says Zephaniah, "seek righteousness, seek humility" (Zeph 2:3). Seeking the Lord, the opposite of self-seeking, forms us in humility. We seek the Lord with a heart purified of pride and ambition, purified of the false security found in riches, of the self-gratification that we seek in sinful pleasures. The more we turn to God in loving trust and hope and detach ourselves from all that is not God, the purer our hearts become. "The pure of heart shall see God."

What then is poverty of spirit? It is far more than material poverty or a simple, frugal lifestyle. It goes beyond detachment from material things such as money and possessions. It is poverty of person. Our very self is poor and needy, and we know it. Poverty of spirit is detachment from self, from pride, from the attempt to be self-sufficient and a law unto self. We do not find our riches in self, in our wisdom or power or wealth, but in God alone.

With the words of Zephaniah, "Seek humility," we have come full circle from our opening chapter, where we saw Zephaniah's definition of the *anawim*, "a people humble and lowly" who "seek refuge in the name of the Lord—the remnant of Israel" (Zeph 3:12).

Pope Pius XI said that Christians "are all spiritual Semites," for Christian spirituality is fully rooted in Jewish spirituality. The beatitudes express the full flowering of Israelite *anawim* spirituality and fully express Christian spirituality. The holy remnant that Zephaniah announced is the people who live the beatitudes.

The *anawim* of old looked for the messiah's coming. The *anawim* of today look for his final coming when he will bring all things together in unity under his headship. The same poverty and trust that prepared Yahweh's poor ones for the messiah's first coming are the only adequate preparation for his final coming. Therefore let us "fulfill all righteousness" (Mt 3:15) by living the beatitudes in the humility and meekness of Jesus, the poor One par excellence.

> Blessed are the poor in spirit, for theirs is the kingdom of heaven.
>
> Blessed are those who mourn, for they will be comforted.
>
> Blessed are the meek, for they will inherit the earth.
>
> Blessed are those who hunger and thirst for righteousness, for they will be filled.
>
> Blessed are the merciful, for they will receive mercy.
>
> Blessed are the pure in heart, for they will see God.
>
> Blessed are the peacemakers, for they will be called children of God.
>
> Blessed are those who are persecuted for righteousness' sake, for theirs is the kingdom of heaven (Mt 5:3–10).

BOOKS & MEDIA

The Daughters of St. Paul operate book and media centers at the following addresses. Visit, call or write the one nearest you today, or find us on the World Wide Web, www.pauline.org

CALIFORNIA
3908 Sepulveda Blvd., Culver City, CA 90230; 310-397-8676
5945 Balboa Ave., San Diego, CA 92111; 858-565-9181
46 Geary Street, San Francisco, CA 94108; 415-781-5180

FLORIDA
145 S.W. 107th Ave., Miami, FL 33174; 305-559-6715

HAWAII
1143 Bishop Street, Honolulu, HI 96813; 808-521-2731
Neighbor Islands call: 800-259-8463

ILLINOIS
172 North Michigan Ave., Chicago, IL 60601; 312-346-4228

LOUISIANA
4403 Veterans Memorial Blvd., Metairie, LA 70006; 504-887-7631

MASSACHUSETTS
Rte. 1, 885 Providence Hwy., Dedham, MA 02026; 781-326-5385

MISSOURI
9804 Watson Rd., St. Louis, MO 63126; 314-965-3512

NEW JERSEY
561 U.S. Route 1, Wick Plaza, Edison, NJ 08817; 732-572-1200

NEW YORK
150 East 52nd Street, New York, NY 10022; 212-754-1110
78 Fort Place, Staten Island, NY 10301; 718-447-5071

OHIO
2105 Ontario Street, Cleveland, OH 44115; 216-621-9427

PENNSYLVANIA
9171-A Roosevelt Blvd., Philadelphia, PA 19114; 215-676-9494

SOUTH CAROLINA
243 King Street, Charleston, SC 29401; 843-577-0175

TENNESSEE
4811 Poplar Ave., Memphis, TN 38117; 901-761-2987

TEXAS
114 Main Plaza, San Antonio, TX 78205; 210-224-8101

VIRGINIA
1025 King Street, Alexandria, VA 22314; 703-549-3806

CANADA
3022 Dufferin Street, Toronto, Ontario, Canada M6B 3T5; 416-781-9131
1155 Yonge Street, Toronto, Ontario, Canada M4T 1W2; 416-934-3440

¡También somos su fuente para libros, videos y música en español!